ST. PAUL'S TEACHING

ON

SANCTIFICATION.

ST. PAUL'S TEACHING

ON

SANCTIFICATION.

A PRACTICAL EXPOSITION OF ROMANS VI.

BY

JAMES MORISON, D.D.,

Author of Practical Commentaries on Matthew, Mark, etc.

WIPF & STOCK · Eugene, Oregon

Wipf and Stock Publishers
199 W 8th Ave, Suite 3
Eugene, OR 97401

St. Paul's Teaching on Sanctification
A Practical Exposition of Romans VI
By Morison, James
ISBN 13: 978-1-62564-380-3
Publication date 10/1/2013
Previously published by Hodder and Stoughton, 1887

PREFACE.

By *Practical Exposition* I do not mean Free and Easy Observations, or Pious Reflections, *carried* '*to*' *the sacred text*, and there suspended on pegs of Scripture Phraseology.

All Scripture-Exposition — inclusive of that which is designated *Practical*—is, or ought to be, Scripture-Explication. It is, or ought to be, the unfolding and exposing-to-view of the thoughts which had been infolded in the origination of the sacred text.

It belongs to the ideal of such Exposition as is fitly called *Practical*, to speak directly to the unprofessional intelligence, and as much as possible in the accredited dialect of culture. When thus speaking the Expositor should present to the public, not so much the processes as the results of scientific exegesis.

Men in masses may be expected to take interest in such literature, when men individually succeed in verifying for themselves the contents of the sacred writings, as constituting a message of ‘good news’ that comes home to every one's ‘business and bosom.’

The topic treated by the Apostle in Romans vi, is certainly exceedingly practical. It is hence all the more likely to take us near and nearer still to the heart of our duties, necessities, and privileges. It is full of counsel to which it would be well were all the world to listen and take earnest heed.

There is not much of special literature connected with Romans vi, in the department either of *Introduction* or of *Exposition*. The Chapter has, on the whole, been found to be, in several of its elements, somewhat perplexing, though profoundly interesting. Then, unlike Chapters v, vii, and ix, it has not, to any appreciable extent, been turned into an arena of theological gladiatorship. There is scope for a good deal of fresh exegesis.

One charm of the Chapter is imperishable:—Its entire contents are the genuine literary product of the Apostle's own mind and heart. The authenticity of the *Epistle to the Romans*, like that of the 'perfervid' *Epistle to the Galatians*, is, by the unanimous verdict of critics, unchallengeable, so that, when we reach the writer's standpoints, we tread the very ground on which the Apostle himself stood, and which he turned into a 'clearing' for our occupation. While we read, and ponder, and reflect, we think some of the choicest of his thoughts.

FLORENTINE BANK HOUSE,
  HILLHEAD, GLASGOW.
    1886.

ST. PAUL'S TEACHING IN ROMANS VI.

V. 1. "*What then shall we say?*" (Τί οὖν ἐροῦμεν;) A transition-expression, and a debater's phrase. It was a favourite with the Apostle, who alone of all the New Testament writers makes use of it. Here it serves as a logical bridge, by means of which his discursive mind passes into a new domain of discussion.

It is the *Ethics of Christianity*, or the *Doctrine of Sanctification* as distinguished from *Justification*, of which the Apostle is about to treat.

He does not feel that it is in a spirit of loneliness that he enters into a consideration of this great and most practical theme. His enthusiasm is infectious; and he is confident that his readers will go along with him, and surge around him, so that unitedly they and he will have fellowship together. Hence the plural expression ἐροῦμεν.

But the writer is not about to isolate the discussion of the great theme. He is not intending to compose a distinct *Dissertation on Sanctifica-*

1

tion, which might be thrust into his doctrinal letter. His discussion is to be part and parcel of a larger discussion on *Christian Salvation*. Hence the illative particle ' *then* ' (οὖν) in the transition-phrase : *What ' then ' shall we say ?* It looks back to the discussion that precedes, and on the crest of which the reader is, with the Apostle himself, carried forward to a doctrinal stage, that is clearly in advance of the positions reached in what goes before. *In view of the discussion immediately preceding, what, in consistency with logical thought, shall we proceed to say ?*

Shall it be, " *Let us persist in sin that grace may increase ?* "   Shall we say that?

Note the substitution, in our translation, of the hortative expression *Let us persist in sin*, for the future expression in King James's Version, *Shall we continue in sin ?*   There can be no doubt that in the Greek text we should, instead of the future ἐπιμενοῦμεν, read the subjunctive ἐπιμένωμεν.   It is the reading of Lachmann, Tischendorf, Tregelles, Westcott-and-Hort ; and it may be rendered either, according to its deliberative usage, *Should we persist in sin ?* or, according to its hortative usage, *Let us persist in sin.*   The two usages coalesce in substantive import.   (See Matt. vi. 31 ; xvii. 4 ; Mark iv. 30 ; 1 Cor. xv. 32.)

It was said in the immediately preceding con-

text that " where sin abounded grace abounded
more exceedingly." The sphere of man's sin was
encompassed by the vaster sphere of God's grace.
While man's sin was exceedingly great, God's
grace was still greater. Man's transgression was
incalculably multiplied by the formal introduction
of the Law (see chap. v. 20); but this multiplication and increase gave occasion to a still greater
multiplication and increase of the grace and compassion of God. Well, *what now shall we say?*
Shall we say this, *Let us persist in sinning that
grace may be multiplied and abound?*

V. 2. " *Far be it.*" (Μὴ γένοιτο.) Let aversion
to such an idea be accentuated to the utmost
degree.

" *How shall we, who died to sin, still live in
it?*" (οἵτινες ἀπεθάνομεν τῇ ἁμαρτίᾳ, πῶς ἔτι ζήσομεν
ἐν αὐτῇ;)

It is assumed that it may be said of all true
Christians, *They once died to sin,* i.e. *in relation
to sin.* The idea is, that, when they became
united to Christ, they died in relation to sin.
In becoming united to Christ, they were united
to Him *in His death.* They were, so to speak,
absorbed into His personality, and thus identified
with Him in His death. His death was theirs.
It was as much theirs as it would have been,

had they, when He died, been literally members
of His body, parts of His person.   They get
the benefit of His death just as if they had
literally endured the dying.   Now, when Christ
died, *He died in relation to sin.*   He died *by it*
indeed.   He also died *on account of it.*   But He
likewise died *to it* ; so that, if human sin should
or could be regarded as impersonated, it would
yet have no farther claims against Him.   Viewed
vicariously, as the representative of sinful men,
Christ was freed, when He died, from farther
penal claims on the part of sin.   And we, who
believe in Him, go back to the same great crisis
of His being and *die with Him.*   Hence the
Apostle says, *we died to sin.*   It is not a state
of sanctification that is described ; it is not *a
daily dying* to the seductive influence of sin that
is referred to.   It is death as the exhaustion of
penalty that is spoken of.   M. le Cene, though
representing quite a host of expositors, is on the
wrong lines entirely when he bodies forth, as the
purport of the first paragraph of this chapter,
the following heading : " *The baptised ought to be
dead to sin for ever.   The new life.*"

But what is the Apostle's argument ?   He
finds in the fact that *we died in Jesus to sin,*
a reason why we should not continue unsanc-
tified, or, as he expresses it, why we should not
" persist in sinning,"—why we should not " live

in sin." The force of the reasoning resolves itself into the might of the motive to holiness, which is involved in the fact that the believer in Christ obtains immunity from the penalty of the sins of which he has been guilty. This immunity is under another phase 'forgiveness.' It is forgiveness for the sake of Christ; forgiveness based on the mediatorial suffering of Christ, as its "meritorious cause." It is forgiveness assured to the believer by his union, through faith, with Christ. The might of the moral motive consists in the magnitude and excellency of the blessing that is realised. "We love Him because He first loved us,"—a wonderful and unspeakable blessing. "She," whose forgiven sins are many, "loveth much." The love of Christ, and of God in Christ, "constraineth the believer to live, not to himself, but to Christ." That is to say, it constrains him to "follow holiness," and to run in the way of God's commandments. *How then shall we, who died to sin, and whose characteristic it is that we thus died (οἵτινες), live any longer in it?* How shall we, who have got forgiveness of sin in so wonderful a way, and at so wonderful a cost, be indifferent in our hearts to the will of God, and give ourselves up to sinning?

V. 3. "*Or*" (ἤ). It is as if the Apostle were
to say, *or, let me put the case somewhat differ-
ently.* There is not much of 'disjunction' in
the Apostle's representations, and nothing of
'antithesis.' Hence Luther, and Tyndale, and
other translators, leave the particle untranslated.
The Vulgate, followed by Erasmus and Beza,
translates it by the Latin '*an.*'

"*Know ye not ?* " ('Αγνοεῖτε;) *Surely it is the
case that ye know.* The Apostle is about to make
a statement, which he expected to be instantly
endorsed by his Roman brethren; and that, not
simply out of their confidence in his present
teaching, but out of the resources of their pre-
vious knowledge in reference to the nature of
Christianity and its institutions.

"*That all we who were baptized into Christ
Jesus,*" (ὅτι ὅσοι ἐβαπτίσθημεν εἰς Χριστὸν Ἰησοῦν,)
i.e. who were united to Christ Jesus by baptism.
The expression εἰς Χριστόν is not to be rendered,
with Oltramare, *in Christ ;* nor, with Meyer, *in
reference to Christ ;* nor, with Darby and the
Geneva, *unto Christ ;* nor, with Beet, *for Christ ;*
nor, with Tyndale, *in the name of Christ.* Luther
and Myles Coverdale give it correctly, *into Christ.*
The phrase is a Pauline idiom, but it simply
denotes inward union with Christ, effected
through inward baptism. That is the Apostle's
idea. He is thinking of such union as qualifies

believers of the gospel for affirming, *we died to sin; we died, namely in Christ.* We needed to be in Christ, in order that in Him we might die to sin. The expression σύμφυτοι γεγόναμεν in v. 5, *we have become grown together,* makes it evident that the Apostle is thinking of the vital union that subsists between Christians and Christ.

How can such a vital union be effected through baptism? Never through the baptism of water. It is a spiritual union. It is a union that is realisable and realised in, for example, holy and consistent members of *the Society of Friends,* although they observe no water-baptism at all. It is realised equally in those who are baptised by immersion, and in those who have been baptised under the form of some other mode. It is a union which is not determined in its date by the date of the administration of the outer ordinance. The baptism of water in infancy does not secure its realisation, either then or at any subsequent period of life. The baptism of water, administered in mature life on the warrant of actual faith and conversion, is an anachronism, if intended to secure vital union with Christ. That vital union is, by hypothesis, already secured. It is therefore quite irrespective of outward baptism. It has been realised by the holy in all ages, and under all dispensations. In no age or dispensation has forgiveness or salvation been, in any single case, realised apart from Christ. It is utterly unrealisable except in union with Christ. The name Christ, and the history of Christ, may not be universally known. But they are known to God. And it is on the footing of what Christ is, and did, and does, that the Great Father deals propitiously with men everywhere, and thus makes known, evangelistically, His propitiousness.

When, then, the Apostle says *we were baptised into Christ Jesus,* he refers exclusively to that spiritual or mystic baptism which has been common to all ages and dispensations, and which is expressly spoken of in Matt. iii. 11, "I indeed baptise you with water unto repentance: but He that cometh after me is mightier than I, whose shoes I am not worthy to bear: *He shall baptise you with the Holy Spirit and with fire.*"

The same distinction is implied in what is written in John i. 26, in answer to the question "Why then baptisest thou, if thou art not the Christ, neither Elijah, nor the prophet?" John answered them saying, "*I baptise with water*: in the midst of you standeth one whom ye know not, even He that cometh after me, the latchet of whose shoe I am not worthy to loose." It

is antithetically implied that the Baptist's great
successor would baptise with something trans-
cendently superior to water. We read again in
the *Acts of the Apostles* i. 4, 5, that Jesus
charged His disciples "to wait for the promise
of the Father, which, said He, ye heard from
Me, for John indeed baptised with water : *but
ye shall be baptised with the Holy Spirit not
many days hence.*" There is then, over and above
the baptism of water, a spiritual baptism. In
its administration there will no doubt be various
aims and adaptations. But if a baptismal influence be indispensable for faith, repentance,
conviction, conversion, sanctification, then doubtless it will not be wanting in the Providence of
God; nor will it be behindhand, when souls
are being savingly united to the Saviour.

There is a statement made by the Apostle in
his first Epistle to the Corinthians, which casts a
clear and steady light upon the passage before us.
It occurs in chap. xii. 12, 13 : " For as the body
is one, and hath many members, and all the
members of the body, being many, are one body;
so also is Christ (viz. in His mystic or ideal
personality); *for in one Spirit were we all
baptised into one body, whether Jews or Greeks,
whether bond or free; and were all made to
drink of one Spirit. For the body is not one
member, but many.*" V. 27. "Now *ye are the*

body of Christ and, severally, the members thereof."

To be *baptised into Christ*, then, is to be united to Him spiritually and vitally by that spiritual influence that baptises souls.

" *Know ye not that as many of us as were baptised into Christ, were baptised into His death ?* " The Apostle is throwing light on the expression in the 2nd verse, " we *died* to sin." Yes, *there is 'death' in the case.* It was primarily *the death of Christ.* But secondarily it is the death of all those who are " in Him." For they, who have been spiritually united to Him by spiritual baptism, have been, by their spiritual baptism, spiritually *united to Him in His death.* Had it not been for *His death* they would never have been united to Him at all. He came into the world to " give His life " as a ransom. He came into our human nature *to " die."* He was delivered up by the determinate counsel and foreknowledge of God that He might " die." His death is the pivot of Christianity. And hence if men are to be in vital union with Him at all, it is fit and meet that they should be *baptised into His " death."*

V. 4. " *We were buried therefore with Him by our baptism into His death."* (συνετάφημεν οὖν αὐτῷ διὰ τοῦ βαπτίσματος εἰς τὸν θάνατον.) Very literally, and un-idiomatically, the statement would run thus: " *We were buried therefore with Him through* ' *the* ' *baptism into* ' *the* ' *death.*" The two articles, before *baptism* and *death* respectively, may, in our English idiom, be fittingly rendered as pro-- nouns. They refer to ' the ' baptism and ' the ' death, which are specified in the immediately preceding context.

It is to be noted that it is not *into Christ's burial* that believers are baptised. It is *into His death*, His crucifixion. (See Gal. ii. 20.)

But the believer's death, like his Lord's, is not an ultimate state or stage. There was to Christ and there is tc us, something beyond death, to which we advar. e. There is much,— much too that is great, and bright, and good. The Apostle, in the striking representation that lies before us, traces the course of our Lord's progressive experience, and of the kindred ex- perience of those who have been baptised into Him.

After death, burial naturally follows. There was burial in the case of our Lord. It was a quiet pause between the pathos of His crucifixion and the triumph of His resurrection. So far as its connection with His decease is concerned, its chief value resolves itself into its evidential relationship. It is evidence of the reality of the death. No mere *swoon*, such as Bunsen conjectured, no mere *lethargy*, such as Schleiermacher fancied, had taken place. Christ literally died and was literally buried. But His burial, like His death, was only a stepping-stone to an ulterior condition. While His body was in the grave, and His soul was in Hades—" the world of the disembodied," He looked calmly forth, anticipating translation to the glory that is beyond, and to the "fulness of joy" that is "for evermore." A corresponding spiritual experience is the prerogative of all His people. In the first moment of their faith they are—so to speak—absorbed into the Saviour's ideal personality. They are "in Him" for participation in the decease which He accomplished. "In Him" they "died to sin," and were thus freed from its penalty on the ground of His vicarious dying. Hence, while consciously realizing this marvellous manifestation of Divine goodness and mercy, they can pause a little for contemplation "aft and afore." They are, for a brief space, put apart and "buried with Christ." The spiritual death is past. The spiritual resurrection is about to be. And meanwhile, between the two there is, in the Christian consciousness, the vital touch and feeling of that link that binds into unity an unspeakably momentous past and an unspeakably momentous future. Hence, in the Apostle's

actual and practical preaching of the gospel, he
went into consecutive detail, and, wherever he
unfurled his blood-stained banner, he proclaimed,
" Christ died for our sins according to the Scriptures: *and He was buried;* and He rose again
the third day according to the Scriptures" (1 Cor.
xv. 3, 4). That announcement, said he, "is the
gospel which I preached " (1 Cor. xv. 1).

"*In order that, as Christ was raised from the
dead by means of the glory of the Father, so we
also might walk-about in newness of life.*" (ἵνα
ὥσπερ ἠγέρθη Χριστὸς ἐκ νεκρῶν διὰ τῆς δόξης τοῦ
πατρός, οὕτως καὶ ἡμεῖς ἐν καινότητι ζωῆς περιπατήσωμεν). This is the end intended by God in our
union with Christ as regards His death, burial,
and resurrection :—*that we should walk-about in
newness of life.* Our Lord's resurrection is rather
assumed than directly asserted. But He did
rise from among the dead and *walk-about.* It
was *newness of life* to Him,—a new state and
style of life. He was no longer exposed to the
penalty of human sin. His agony was past.
The whole confluence of sufferings that dragged
their slow length along the career of His humili-
ation, and that finally discharged themselves into
His agony, and then into His crucifixion, and
thence into the sacrificial surrender of His life
when "His heart was broken," *—all this had

* See Stroud's *Physical Cause of Christ's Death.* 2nd Edit.

passed away for ever. There were to be no more hidings of His Father's countenance behind the accumulated fogs and clouds of human sins. Never again would there be, to the sensibility of His heart, a feeling as of dereliction. The joy of absolute complacency had arisen in His soul, like a sun, and was hasting to its eternal zenith. It was the life of infinite bliss, on which our Lord had, in His humanity, entered. It was "glorification."

Somewhat similar is the new life of believers; only it is but in epitome and miniature. They walk-about in this world as heirs of the world that is to come,—the world of glory. All good things are theirs. They are heirs of God and joint heirs with Christ :—so great, so grand is their heritage. Their very trials are turned into blessings and made to work together for their good. (See Rom. viii. 28.)

The believer's *newness of life*, as is evidenced by our Lord's *newness of life*, is not a peculiarity of ethical character, but a peculiarity of personal privilege and estate.

It was *by the glory of the Father* that the Saviour was raised from among the dead. There was the occurrence of *a glorious exertion of power*. The power employed was the Father's; though in no such exclusive sense as to debar the co-operation of the Son (John ii. 19). As the Supreme

Magistrate of the universal moral empire, the Father was most emphatically well-pleased with the self-sacrifice of the Son. And hence " *He* raised Him up, having loosed the pains of death " (Acts ii. 24). " This Jesus *did God raise up,* whereof "—says St. Peter—" we all are witnesses " (Acts ii. 32). " Ye killed the Prince of Life "—said the same Apostle again—"*whom God raised from the dead,* whereof we are witnesses " (Acts iii. 15). He says again in chapter iv. 10, " Whom God *raised from the dead.*" St. Peter thus agrees with St. Paul in ascribing the eventuation of the Saviour's resurrection to " the glory of the Father."

The believer in Christ, who has realised his union with the Saviour in *death* and *burial,* will, without difficulty, or hesitancy, still farther realise his union in *resurrection,* pregnant, as that resurrection is, with " newness of life " and " joy that is unspeakable and full of glory."

When the Apostle says " we were *therefore* buried," the " *therefore* " links the *burial* to the preceding *death,* and leaves it to be inferred that there is, in Christian experience, another link in advance that unites to *resurrection-life.*

V. 5. This is an exceedingly compressed verse. The ideas are crowded and, as it were, crammed together, with the effect of so inter-twisting the phraseology that very careful analysis is required.

The original Greek runs thus, Εἰ γὰρ σύμφυτοι γεγόναμεν τῷ ὁμοιώματι τοῦ θανάτου αὐτοῦ, ἀλλὰ καὶ τῆς ἀναστάσεως ἐσόμεθα.

The *For* or γάρ indicates that the Apostle desires to confirm the declaration, that it is divinely contemplated that we, who believe in Christ, should walk-about in newness of life. "*For if*— says he—*we have become united with Him in death, we shall assuredly be united with Him in His resurrection likewise.*"

The word σύμφυτοι, *grown together*, in its relation to περιπατήσωμεν, *that we should walk-about*, exhibits a marked mixture of metaphors, which a fastidious rhetorician would not unlikely have avoided. The idea, however, is sufficiently transparent. Believers *have become grown together with Christ*. The translation of the Vulgate is free, *si conplantati facti sumus*. The Rheims translation is, *if we be become complanted;* and, accordantly, that of our public English version is, *if we have been planted together*. The Geneva is, *if we be grafted with Him*. Tyndale's is simply *if we be graft*. But σύμφυτοι is rather *grown together*, than either *planted* or *graffed together*. The real idea is, *intimately united*, so intimately as to be *vitally one*. Such is the relation of

Christians to Christ. They have become *intimately and vitally united to Him in His death.* And, says the Apostle, if this be the case, as it really is, then it follows that they shall be also intimately and vitally united to Him in His resurrection. Death without resurrection would be, to Christ, but one-half of the arch of His glory, a fragment riven off and torn from the unity of His mediatorial enterprise. It would be as a hemisphere of impenetrable gloom, with no hemisphere of light and lustre beyond, like day succeeding night, or sunshine after storm. To Christ the resurrection was indispensable, unless death, darkness, and defeat were to be the ultimate condition and fate of the universe. But if resurrection be to Christ an ethical necessity and an assured reality, then its bright and blissful issue will be part and parcel of the joint-heirship of believers. " If they be united to Christ in His death, *then they will be likewise united to Him in His resurrection.*" It is a finely pictorial, or hieroglyphical, and figurative way of saying, that if deliverance from the woful penal effects of sin be assured, through Christ, to those who believe in Him as their Saviour, so will be their admission into participation with Him of the glorious reward of His perfect offering of righteousness.

The Apostle, however, does not simply say, *if we have become intimately united with Him*

c

in His death, so shall we also be in His resurrec-
tion ; he introduces the idea of *likeness* (ὁμοίωμα),
and says, *if we have become most intimately*
united with Him in the 'likeness' of His death,
so shall we also be in that of His resurrec-
tion. It is two distinct representations which
he welds together. The one we have been
considering ; the other is to the effect that *if*
we have become 'like' to Christ in death, so shall
we be in resurrection.

Likeness to Christ in death is distinguished
from *identification.* It is a difference in ideal
representation. But both views are admirably
harmonious with the concrete reality to which
they are applied. Believers of the gospel can
say of themselves, *we died in Christ to sin.* Here
is identification. But they can likewise say,
our death to sin is 'like' the death of Christ to
sin. Here is similitude.

There is scope for this representation of
similitude. Christ's death to sin was both outward and inward in its peculiarity. It was both
physical and spiritual. But the believer's death
to sin is inward only, and spiritual. The two
representations are not identical, but like. Each
of the deaths represented is a death to sin.
The real idea is, that for the sake of the death
of Christ there is deliverance from the penalty
of sin. There is what is equivalent to pardon.

And if there be, then there is likewise something more. There is life, positive life. There is the fulness of bliss in expectancy. There is the inheritance of glory and honour coupled with immortality (Romans ii. 7–10).

The ἀλλά or *but*, that leads the ' apodosis ' of the sentence, is the survival of a fuller representation that had hovered in the mind of the writer : " If we were united with Him in the likeness of His death, *that will not be the full extent of the union ; but* we shall be also united in the likeness of His resurrection."

The future ἐσόμεθα, *we shall be*, is not intended to be historically predictive. It simply denotes a relation of logical sequence. If union in the death of Christ be postulated, *it follows* that union in His resurrection may likewise be assumed. He who is sure of the first phase of union has equal reason to be sure of the other.

V. 6. "*Knowing this*" (τοῦτο γινώσκοντες). The *this*, the τοῦτο, is prospective, pointing forward to the statements lying on the other side of the verb γινώσκοντες. The participle introduces a clear subjective certainty, that is additional to the assurance that is involved in the hypothetical proposition of the preceding verse : " *knowing this that our old man was crucified with* (*Him*)."

(ὅτι ὁ παλαιὸς ἡμῶν ἄνθρωπος συνεσταυρώθη.) By the expression *our old man* the Apostle means *our former self, our self such as we were before conversion.* The phrase is relative to the antithetic phrase *the new man.* See Eph. iv. 22-24; Col. iii. 9, 10. In consequence of this reciprocal relativity of the two phrases, neither of them is strictly applicable or realisable in the case of the unconverted. It is the presence of *the new man* that turns the other self into *the old man.* The word *old* in the phrase does not mean *aged;* and *new* is not *youthful* or *young.* There are shreds, indeed, of these meanings in the two terms. But *the old man* is the former unconverted self; *the new man* is the man that is the present and converted self. The representation must not be pared to the quick. In the Epistles to the Ephesians and the Colossians the will-endowed self-hood of Christian believers is represented as acting, or as having acted, in reference to both the old and the new self-hood, as if there were three self-hoods in the unity of the one personality. But of course the self-hood is only one. And the old and new self-hoods are but the subjective or ideal relativities of the personal unity.

The believer's former self was — says the Apostle—*crucified with Christ.* The idea is that on the occurrence of faith in Christ, as Christ is revealed in the gospel, a union supervened. The man was taken up "into Christ" so as to be "in Christ." The glorious Being, who was the object of the man's faith, absorbed him into His Crucified Self. Such and so intimate was their union. As far as resultant privileges were concerned, the crucifixion belonged to the sinner as well as to the Sufferer. The man was " crucified with Christ." He was no sharer—so far as consciousness was concerned—of the pangs of penal crucifixion as endured on Calvary. But he enjoyed the immunity, consequent on the exhaustion of the penalty, just as if he had been literally crucified in Christ.

The Apostle says *our old man was crucified.* The representation is a variation from that which is found in Galatians ii. 20, " I have been crucified with Christ, and I no longer live, but Christ liveth in me." The Christ-element in the life of the Apostle was supreme. But in the passage before us it is not at all the present life of the Apostle or his peers that is referred to. *It is the old man who is represented as co-crucified.* Crucifixion with Christ is not the antecedent, it is the consequent, of ' saving faith.' There is not, first, conscious union with Christ, and then faith. The order is the reverse of that. It is first faith, and then union with Christ. But union with Christ is essential to immunity from sin's penalty and to the inheritance of glory and honour coupled with immortality. It is not, first, immunity and inheritance, and then union with Christ. It is, first, union with Christ and then immunity and inheritance. It is " in Christ " that we get pardon, justification, and glorification. Hence it is *the old man* that was co-crucified with Christ. There was no *new man* till the co-crucifixion was consummated.

But why this crucifixion of the old man with Christ? Why should there be any such union with Christ? What is the grand aim? the " final cause" ? Is it that believers of the gospel, attaining the specified union with all its immunities and prospective inheritances, may rest for ever and be thankful? Is it that their self-hood may be filled and gorged with unlimited gratification? *Away for ever be the thought!* (Mὴ γένοιτο.) Such selfism would be selfishness in infinite degree. It is an end that would be utterly unworthy of both God and man. And far other was the conception of the Apostle. He explains his teleology thus : " *in order that the body of sin might be utterly disabled, so that it may no longer be able to tyrannise over us* (ἵνα καταργηθῇ τὸ σῶμα τῆς ἁμαρτίας, τοῦ μηκέτι δουλεύειν ἡμᾶς τῇ ἁμαρτίᾳ). Such is God's aim in our co-crucifixion with Christ. The Apostle's representation is highly figurative. He thinks

of sin as a tyrant. It rules the sinner with a
rod of iron. It is with no gentle hand that it
wields its massive sceptre. The tyrant is hard
and harsh. The Apostle ascribes to it a *body*.
It is the vehicle of the tyrant's tyranny. All
the members are sedulously, unfeelingly, cruelly
employed in carrying out his unreasoning and
unreasonable will. But it is in vain that expositors debate with one another what this *body*
realistically is. The Apostle is drawing on the
canvas of his imagination the picture of a tyrant.
He is thinking, for the moment, in the figures
of a fertile fancy. Every tyrant has a body of
one description or other, and tyrannises in it and
through it. But let us not abandon the Apostle's
generic idealism for a narrowly specific or in-
dividualising representation.

Christianity has to do with this *body of sin*.
The end contemplated in reference to it is *that
it might be mortally disabled.* Hence the co-
crucifixion. When *the old man* is crucified with
Christ, *the body of sin*, as ensphered within him,
is transfixed upon the cross. The figures are
not drawn with absolute literary nicety and art.
The Apostle is not seeking for "the wisdom of
words." *The old man* and *the body of sin* are
in reality, as he draws them, not perfectly identical in character. The *new man* has special relations to each; and thus, in both cases a difference

is involved. There is, however, on either side of the involution the 'promise and the potency' of a grand final result. That is the burden of the doctrinal import. And hence, when the Apostle speaks of the union of believers with the Saviour, a union in virtue of which His immunities and prospective privileges become theirs, the language conveys the assurance that the union will be regulated and dominated by an aim grandly ethical and Divine. The aim is this, that by the might of matchless generosity and loving-kindness on the part of God, the delusive and seductive power of sin may, on the part of men, be broken in their hearts. Men's " sanctification" is God's aim; and His principal ethical leverage within the heart is the noble principle of gratitude for grace received.

Καταργηθῆ. This picturesque term is one of the Apostle's favourites, and is here rendered in the authorized English Version, *might be destroyed*. In no other author, sacred or secular, is the term wielded with so much zest. It means *to render idle, to make inefficient or inoperative, to disable*. It reveals that it is part and parcel of the Divine ethical aim to break the power of sin. To the believing, sin is like a crucified tyrant. It may linger on for a period, and, by force of habit, authority may be conceded to it for a limited time; but its power is mortally broken. Soon must it altogether cease to annoy or deceive. It is doomed; and by and by it will be "brought to nought."

Καταργέω is rendered *to destroy* in 1 Cor. vi. 13; xv. 26; 2 Thess. ii. 8; Heb. ii. 14. It is rendered *to abolish* in 2 Cor. iii. 13; Eph. ii. 15; 2 Tim. i. 10. Sin will yet be *abolished* and *destroyed*.

What henceforward is the relation of believers to the tyrant? The Apostle reveals the Divine aim, "*that so we should no longer be in bondage to sin*" (τοῦ μηκέτι δουλεύειν ἡμᾶς τῇ ἁμαρτίᾳ). There had been already too much bondage. The tyrant had got his own way too long. And the poor serfs had not had the manliness to strike off their fetters when they had the power. They were willing to be slaves, leading a grovelling life, and refusing to be free. The moral infatuation was profound.

Such was the condition of men everywhere when the Divine Deliverer appeared on the scene. He struck a blow for freedom, that has been, all down through the ages, reverberated in millions of human hearts, and in millions more. He died in the conflict; but He triumphed as He died, and by His dying. He took men up with Him into His death, so that they were co-crucified. And the grand ethical aim of the Great God was *that the body of sin might be utterly disabled, so that they should be no longer in bondage to sin*.

The category of time must in some respects be merged in the Apostle's representation. The old man *was* co-crucified. The old man *is* co-crucified. The union between Christ and Christians *was.* And it *is.*

Since the life and death of Jesus have entered into the historical evolution of the human race, there is Divine provision, available to all men, for emancipation from the penalty, as also, and thence, for emancipation from the degradation and folly of sin. Such was, such is, the ethical aim of the Great God. And such is the substrate of import in the verse we have been considering.

V. 7. "*For he who died has been justified from his sin.*" ('Ο γὰρ ἀποθανὼν δεδικαίωται ἀπὸ τῆς ἁμαρτίας.) The Apostle reiterates the great evangelical blessing conferred upon the believer—the blessing that carries in its bosom the grand motive power for sanctification. *The believer has been justified from his sin.* The Apostle's *for*, or γάρ, should be noticed. It confirms the immediately preceding statement concerning the believer's privilege. The discourse is dialectically knit together, but not simply with a bare sufficiency of rigidly logical coherence. The writer recurs with epistolary freedom to the details of his theme, and adds *ex abundanti* link to link.

Ὁ ἀποθανών, *is qui mortuus est*, *he who died*, namely *in Christ*. See both the preceding and the succeeding context. It is the Christian believer who is referred to. His spiritual hopes repose upon the fact of his union with Christ. And the Christ with whom he is in unison and union is *the Christ who died*, He is "Christ the crucified." The believer thinks of Him as such; and still as such he thinks of Him, and has faith in Him. Remove, indeed, *Christ the Crucified* from the believer's faith, and there remains a mere and empty husk of thought. But when the act of faith is present, and likewise the great object, namely, *Christ the Crucified*, then the conditions are present that warrant the identification, in ethical privilege, of the believer and his Lord. Hence the remarkable expression, *he has been justified from his sin*: (δεδικαίωται ἀπὸ τῆς ἁμαρτίας). The idea of *liberation* is subsumed in the idea of *justification*. Hence the ἀπό, or 'from.' A similar subsumption is found in Acts xiii. 39: "and by Christ every one who believeth is *justified from all things*, from which he could not be justified by the law of Moses." The sinner who has—through faith—died with Christ, or who has—through faith—got into union with Christ, is *judicially freed* from the power of sin to condemn to the endurance of sin's penalty. His title to the inheritance of bliss is, notwith-

standing his sins, judicially assured to him. He
is judicially vindicated, and thus justified as one
having in his possession the "righteousness"
which is the sinner's all-sufficient plea. (See
Rom. ix. 30; x. 3-8; iii. 21, 22; i. 16, 17.) The
old Authorized Version of the memorable affirmation of the Apostle entirely hides out of sight the
judicial character of the act that is signalised.
It leaves indeterminate the nature of the *freedom*
asserted.   Is it *the freedom of justification* or *the
freedom of sanctification*, to which the Apostle
refers?   His own Greek leaves no room for
doubt.   He speaks here of *justification*, not of
sanctification, though of *justification* as leading
to *sanctification*.

V. 8.   The Apostle passes on to look at his
fascinating subject from another 'coign of
vantage.'   Hence the initial δέ is, as Meyer
remarks, 'metabatic.'   It is *transitive*, and *effects
transition*.   We have no better rendering for it
in English than our imperfect *but*, and this is the
rendering given in the Revised Version, replacing
the less perspicuous *now* of the Old Version.
Tyndale and the Geneva have *therefore;* Wycliffe
and the Rheims have *and;* Luther has *but*
(aber); and so has the Vulgate (*autem*); and so
has Myles Coverdale.

" *But if we died with Christ* "—a better translation than that of King James's Version, *if we be
dead with Christ.* The Apostle views the death of
believers as an event, not as a continuous state.
But the distinct relations of the category of
time are held by him in abeyance. Believers
died with Christ, but not necessarily at the
historic moment of Christ's own historic death.
Believers died with Christ at the moment when
first they were vitally united to Him. They
were vitally united to Christ at the moment when
they believed the gospel concerning Him. *It
was then, therefore, that they died.* It was then
that they became co-crucified. When we speak
of believers who are at present on the scene of
life, and who have only now, as the spiritual
children of a day, or an hour, or of a moment,
" come to the knowledge of the truth " ; then
we may say, with reference to the event that has
occurred in the crisis-moment of their spiritual
experience, *they have died with Christ: they are
crucified with Christ.*

The Apostle, when saying of himself and his
brethren, *but we died in Christ,* does not go back
in thought, and date from the historic decease of
our Lord, as an event now remote in the area
of things past. He only goes back to the epoch
of the personal experience of himself and his
brethren; and finding that in the consciousness

of that experience the clock of advancing time had struck, he does not say *we die*, except when merely narrating the logical sequence of events, but *we died*. We died *with* Christ.

"*But if we died with Him, we believe that we shall also live with Him.*" (εἰ δὲ ἀπεθάνομεν σὺν Χριστῷ, πιστεύομεν ὅτι καὶ συνζήσομεν αὐτῷ.)

The reference is not to the "life" that was terminated by our Lord's death,—the wonderful "life" that was spent on earth amid men's sorrows and sins. It is to the "life" that, succeeding His death, replaced it, burst its bonds, and utterly "abolished" it. The Apostle speaks of our Lord's *resurrection-life;* and he says that if we were united to the Saviour in His death, we believe that we shall also be united with Him in His resurrection-life.

He employs the future tense, *we shall live*, because the fact of Christ's resurrection is one thing, and His "resurrection-life" is another. The fact of the resurrection transpired on earth and was the event of a moment. The resurrection-life runs on continuously from age to age, and yet to farther ages of ages. It is to us in the future. It is the object of our hope as long as we live (Rom. viii. 24). It is "reserved in heaven for us" (1 Pet. i. 4); and our prospect is to be "for ever with the Lord." The heavens have "received Him," and will "retain Him," "until the time of the restitution of all things" (Acts iii. 21). When the fragile terrestrial tabernacle ceases to be habitable, the emancipated spirit, being "absent from the body," ascends to be "present with the Lord" (2 Cor. v. 1–12). The holy patriarchs, and all Christian pilgrims who have gone on before, "looked for a country." "They sought a city which hath foundations, whose architect and builder is God" (Heb. xi. 10, 14). It is there where Christ is; and it is there where believers of God's gladdening evangel, and just because they give credence to its message of mercy, hope to be. "For," as says the Apostle, "if we died with Christ, we believe that we shall also live with Him." Divine consistency in mercy is the warrant for the assured belief. The blessing that is conferred, in virtue of union with Christ in His death, would be incomplete and fragmentary without the blessing that is conferred in virtue of union with Christ in His resurrection-life. Our union indeed with Christ, in His death, is security for our immunity from the wages of our iniquity. *We died to sin.* But this death is only half the blessing required for human bliss. It is merely the arrest and negation of merited penalty. Is there to be no loving-kindness and tender-mercy beyond? No heaven? No glory and honour coupled with immortality? No participation with Christ in the reward of His spotless righteousness and perfect self-sacrifice? Are we not to rise with Christ and soar into "the heavenlies"? Are we not to be "made to sit with Him"? and to "reign with Him"? Are there not "pleasures for evermore" at the right hand of the Majesty, enough for Christ, enough for us too "in Christ"? Does not the full river of God carry water of life sufficient to quench the thirst of every longing soul? The Apostle reasons that if the negative blessing be generously conferred, the positive will not be grudgingly withheld. If in Christ we die as regards the endurance of the penalty of our sins, in the same Christ we shall live as regards the enjoyment of the reward of His righteousness. If in the case of Christ Himself it would be utterly unnatural to break off abruptly the sequence of resurrection-life from the crisis of His atoning death, not more truly incomplete and unnatural would it be to render us participants in our Saviour's death while withholding from us participation in the glory of His subsequent life. There should be consummation as well as commencement. Christ should be to us, in the matter of our spiritual experience, omega as well as alpha.

V. 9. "*For we know.*" (εἰδότες.) It is as if the

writer were to say—*yes, we shall continuously live mith Him*, subject to no fears of interruption to the life that is lived, "*for we know that Christ, being raised from the dead, dieth no more; death hath no more dominion over Him.*" It was fitting that He should die. He came into our dislocated human world that He might suffer in the friction and die. From the moment that His Divine consciousness dipped down into, and blended with, His human consciousness, He saw looming in the distance the tokens of absolute self-sacrifice. His heart beat funeral marches toward a goal of endurance, that could not be farther postponed, or longer sustained. It was the climax of innocent suffering, and will never be repeated. *Christ being raised from the dead, dieth no more; death has no farther claim on His endurance; it has dominion over Him no more.* What then is our prospect? We shall see.

V. 10. "*For in that He died, He died unto sin once; but in that He liveth, He liveth unto God.*" (ὃ γὰρ ἀπέθανεν, τῇ ἁμαρτίᾳ ἀπέθανεν ἐφάπαξ.) The ὃ is, of course, the accusative of the relative pronoun, although it is peculiarly and emphatically tilted up at the commencement of the sentence. *For what He died,* that is, *for the thing which He died,* and that is,

for the death which He died. The Greeks, like
the English, could speak of *living a life, and
dying a death.* The relative pronoun in the
Apostle's conception is, notwithstanding the ab-
sence of the anticipative μέν, oppositive to the
ὁ δέ in the next clause. *For the death which
on the one hand He died, He died to sin; but
the life which on the other hand He lives, He
lives to God.* The Saviour's death indeed was a
death *by sin;* but that, as we have already seen
(v. 2), is not the Apostle's idea here, nor does
he here mean that the Saviour's death was *for
sin* or *on account of sin.* His idea is this—*Our
Saviour died 'to' sin;* and He thus died *once
for all.* The conception of sin as a tyrant is still
looming over the mind and heart of the writer,
and swaying his representation (see v. 6). The
tyranny of sin is the oldest of all the tyrannies;
and the direst. All men have suffered severely
in consequence. They have been ruthlessly mis-
used as serfs and slaves, and beasts of burden
(Matt. xi. 28). The degradation that is the effect
of sin is immeasurable; correspondingly incommensurable is the woe. Hence the compassion
of God, and the mission of the Saviour. When
the Saviour came into our nature, and became, as
far as might be, our Surety and our Substitute,
He was at once rough-handled by our tyrannous
sin. He was " wounded for our transgressions;

He was bruised for our iniquities." "He was oppressed and He was afflicted." "His visage was marred more than any man, and His form more than the sons of men" (Isa. lii. 14; liii. 5, 7). It was as if blood-hounds had been let loose on Him. The leash of the blood-hound-spirit was let slip. Our Saviour was truculently hunted down as one not fit to live. He died. But in the very act of dying He conquered and triumphed. For He did not merely die. *He died ' to ' sin.* He died *' to ' the sin that sought to murder Him.* By His death He became free from all farther inflictions on account of sin, and all liabilities of the nature of woe. He became free for ever from all farther contact with sin's tyranny or penalty. The idea of *freedom* is ineradically inherent in the representation. Christ entered into a far higher plane of freedom than what is described by the patriarch Job, when he says of the state of death—" There the wicked cease from troubling, and there the weary be at rest; there the prisoners rest together; they hear not the voice of the oppressor; the small and great are there: and the slave is free from his lord" (iii. 17–19). The freedom, into which Christ was introduced when He died to sin, was, unlike the freedom described by Job, realised in consciousness; and was and is available to all, who, groaning under degrading servitude, are

willing and eager to be free. The freedom thus
obtained is for perpetuity. Its "meritorious
cause" is indiminishable in merit; and hence,
as well as for other reasons, "the death which
Christ died, He died *once for all.*"

It is on a different but affiliated line of representation · that the writer of the Epistle to the
Hebrews says, "By His own blood he entered
' *once for all* ' into the Holy Place, having obtained eternal redemption" (chapter ix. 12).

The Apostle, turning to the other side of his
subject, says, *but the life which He is living, He is
living to God* (ὁ δὲ ζῇ, ζῇ τῷ Θεῷ). The death
signalised in the preceding clause was a momen-
tary event; the contradistinguished life is a thing
of continuity. It has been, and is, and will be;
running on from age to age. It is Christ's
resurrection-life (see verse 9). He is living it *to
God.* Although it is the case that He really died
and was dead; yet it is likewise, and as really, the
case, that He is alive, and alive to God. In the
life, which He lived in our nature before He died,
He was doomed to die. Death was imminent all
along His career. It impended, loweringly, over
His head and heart. He was unavoidably ob-
noxious to it. Having clothed Himself in the
garb of our humanity, He had to suffer in it
on account of our human sin. There was no
alternative, if salvation was ever to be achieved

and enjoyed. Hence He patiently endured the appointed suffering, till it culminated in the endurance of a violent death, to which He succumbed on Calvary. In the article of that death, He drained to its dregs the bitter cup of human liability on account of sin; and having drained it, He died. He "tasted death for every man" (Heb. ii. 9). In dying, He died, not to God, but to sin: He was freed for ever,—not from God—but from sin and from all judicial exactions on account of sin.

Hence He lives. Not indeed *to the tyrant sin*, to be exposed to those tyrannous inflictions which are in accordance with the very nature of sin and tyranny. He lives a far other style of life. *He lives to God.* Cognizance is taken of him in the conscious observation of God, who knew the end from the beginning, and who in truth raised Him up from among the dead; and was thereupon ready to deal with Him, and act by Him, in accordance with his peerless Messianic and Redemptive deserts.

Within the sphere of the life that preceded His death, Christ had to do with the liabilities of sin. But within the sphere of the life that succeeded His death, His resurrection-life, He had and has to do with the fruition of those rewards of righteousness which it is joy to the heart of the Righteous Ruler of the universe to confer.

In the expression, *alive to God*, it is not the Saviour's ethical character that is described. It is the fact of the continuance of His mediatorial life. Though He died and disappeared from the observation of men; yet death did not end Him, nor did it hide Him from God. He rose into "newness of life," and lived on with God. He lived and still lives *to God*. If there be non-believers and disbelievers to whom He is Nothing, and who consequently care for none of His things, the loss is theirs. They are coming, in consequence of their culpable ignorance, into collision with realities which are as stable as the foundations of the Universe. Christ, though dead, is living. Yea, He is living because He died. He is living His resurrection-life. God is taking cognizance of Him and rewarding Him with the "fulness of joy," that is reached by "the path of life" (Psa. xvi. 11). Our Saviour is thus living to God, because He died to sin. He has been exalted into the highest glory of "life eternal," because, though "being in the form of God, He counted it not a prize to be on an equality with God, but emptied Himself, taking the form of a servant, being made in the likeness of men; and, being found in fashion as a man, He humbled Himself, becoming obedient even unto death, yea the death of the cross." (Phil. ii. 6, 8).

V. 11. "*So*" (Οὕτως). A spiritual parallelism
is opened up to the mind of the writer. "*Reckon*
ye also yourselves to be dead indeed to sin, but
alive to God through Jesus Christ our Lord" (καὶ
ὑμεῖς λογίζεσθε ἑαυτοὺς εἶναι νεκροὺς μὲν τῇ ἁμαρτίᾳ
ζῶντας δὲ τῷ Θεῷ ἐν Χριστῷ ᾽Ιησοῦ). *Do ye, on your*
part, reckon yourselves. There is a parallelism
between the spiritual state of Christ and the
spiritual state of those who are vitally united to
Him (see ver. 5). The Apostle deemed it a matter of moment that they should realise the fact.
Christ on His part died to sin and lives to God.
Do ye on your part—says the Apostle exhortingly
to his brethren—*consider yourselves to be dead to*
sin, and alive to God in Christ Jesus. Their state
—in virtue of their union with Christ Jesus—was
pre-eminently one of privilege ; and the Apostle
desired that they should realise it as such. Their
sanctification to a large extent, depended on the
realisation.

Consider yourselves to be dead on the one hand
to sin, and alive on the other to God, in Christ
Jesus. The expression *in Christ Jesus* conditions
both of the preceding clauses, and not merely
the latter of the two, as Rückert and Köllner
suppose. It is *in Christ Jesus* that we are *dead*
to sin, just as really as it is in Him that we are
alive to God.

In Christ Jesus dead to sin ! In what respect ?

Not, as has been too often supposed, in respect
to character or ethical demeanour. What then ?
In respect to freedom from penal liability. The
state described is indeed a stepping-stone to
an all-important result in character. But it is
not itself that result.   It is in Christ Jesus
that believers are *dead to sin*, because it is in
virtue of their connection with Him by faith,
that they are in such a state of union with Him,
as regards His meritorious death, that the immunity from future suffering for sin, which is
His by desert, becomes theirs by grace. The
word *dead* is in the Apostle's expression, because
of the peculiar significance of the *death* of our
Lord in the great economy of salvation.   The
very essential principle of the Gospel is that
Christ "*died* for our sins and rose again"
(1 Cor. xv. 3, 4). "In due time Christ *died* for
the ungodly " (Rom. v. 6). " God commendeth
His love toward us in that while we were yet
sinners, Christ *died* for us" (Rom. v. 8). "We
are justified by His *blood*" (Rom. v. 9), and,
 " We were reconciled to God by the *death* of
His Son" (Rom. v. 10). "I," says our Lord,
"*if I be lifted up from the earth* will draw all
men unto me ; this He said signifying what
death He should die" (John xii. 32, 33).   No
wonder therefore that the Apostle so manipu-
lated and moulded his phrases that he inserted

the word '*dead*' into one of the most significant
of them.   Believers are warranted and encou-
raged to " reckon themselves to be *dead to sin.*"
They are thus to reckon themselves " in Christ
Jesus"; and it is because of His singular self-
sacrifice in taking the place of the guilty, and
stooping to *the abasement of death*, even " the
death of the cross " (Phil. ii. 8), that there is
" in Christ Jesus " deliverance from the fatal
" wrath that is to come."

"*And living to God*" (ζῶντας δὲ τῷ Θεῷ).   This
is not something in antithesis to the statement in
the preceding clause.   And hence, in our English
idiom, it is preferable to connect the two statements with the conjunction *and*, rather than with
the somewhat oppositive *but*.   They who are *dead
in relation to sin* are, for that very reason, not
absolutely *dead*, but *alive* or *living in relation to
God*.   Death in relation to sin is entirely consistent with life in relation to God.   The one relationship is complementive of the other.   And both are
charged with mighty moral motive-power, constraining to holiness of conduct and character.

When the Apostle says, *reckon yourselves* ' *alive*'
he does not think of life apart from Christ.   It
is " life *in* Christ Jesus " of which he speaks,
and which he desired his disciples to realise.
" If," says he, " we died with Christ, we believe
that we shall also *live with Him.*"   It is Christ

who is our life. He and He only is the living
" Meritorious Cause " of our bliss.

When speaking of the relation of Christ to
life, we might refer either to the life which He
lived before His death,—a life of ineffable goodness and ethical glory; or we might refer to
the life which He has been living since His
death,—a life of incommensurable exaltation in
glory and honour. It is to this latter life, the
award of the Father to the Son, and thence the
gift of the Son to the multitude of His 'brethren,'
that the Apostle refers. The life spoken of is
the life consequent on the Saviour's crucifixion.
Let all Christians reckon themselves as its
participants. God takes note of the vital in-
terlinking relationship, and acknowledges its
validity. And hence it matters little that some
men deny the reality of the life, " hid " as it is
" with Christ in God." God owns it; and its
beneficiaries enjoy it. No amount of confident
denial, or subtle reasoning, or bitter scorning, or
cruel persecution, or obloquy, can deprive them
of that of which they are conscious.

If the disciples referred to had been ' *dead* '
in relation to God, instead of ' *alive*,' the case
would have been far other and lamentable.
They would have been destitute of the power
of recipiency that is needful in order to take
advantage of Divine blessings.

But not only is God Himself in His essential nature, the *living* God who has *life* in and for Himself; He also has had, and yet has, and ever will have, " life " to give. He had it to give to His Son in infinite plenitude. " For as the Father hath life in Himself, even so gave He to the Son also to have life in Himself " (John v. 26). The Son has received as the Father gave, and hence the life that is in Him is all-sufficient, in plenitude, for the life of men. God the Father gives, and God the Son too. The " fulness of the Godhead " is in the Son, in order that " out of His fulness we all may receive grace for grace." Hence, " God so loved the world that He gave His only begotten Son, that whosoever believeth in Him should not perish but *have everlasting life* " (John iii. 16). They who have the Son " have life," and are " alive to God." Whatever they may be to men around them, however ignored and spurned as Nobodies or as " Things that are not," still before God they live, and will live for ever.

The thought of such inestimable privilege should not be stowed away into the dim recesses and unconsciousnesses of the mind. Contrariwise, the blessings involved should be held forth to catch and reflect the clearest sunlight that can get admission into the human intelligence. The benefits are fraught with remarkably transformative moral potency,—potency that can turn the whole manhood of a man into "a new creation," and convert his surroundings, far as his ethical influence extends, from a waste state of wilderness and weeds into a scene of beauty, budding all over, and blossoming "like the rose." In other words, there is provision for "the beauty of holiness" in the experience of all who, through faith in the Gospel, take home to their hopes and their hearts the blessings of pardon and eternal life.

V. 12. "*Let not sin then reign.*" The inferential conjunction '*then*' turns back the attention to the scope of the preceding discussion; and fittingly introduces the cardinal subject of "sanctification," in its logical sequence to the subject of the lofty privileges as to state, which are assured to those who are "in Christ Jesus."

"Let not sin reign." Sin is again personified (ver. 6), and represented as a sovereign. It cannot sway its sceptre, however, without the consent of the manhood of the man. That manhood may, in self-degrading folly, vote sin into the throne of its being. Or, it may dethrone the usurping tyrant, and come under the sway of a reign, at once most righteous and most benign. A reign, however, of one kind or another there must be. Every man, whether he think it or not, must be subject to some regnant principle and personality. But having free-will, man may choose his king. Hence the Apostle's exhortation, *Let not sin reign.*

There is no latent antithesis between *reigning* and *existing.* The antithesis that is subtended is between the *reigning of sin,* and the *reigning of righteousness* or of the *righteous God.* It should be noticed that the imperative μὴ βασιλευέτω, *let it not reign,* is addressed grammatically to sin, but in doctrinal import to the believer.

" *In your mortal body.*" This is the domain of the royal ruler, whoever he may be. There is significance in the word " *mortal.*" It indicates that " the time is short," and it would therefore be folly and a shame if it were to be wasted and squandered.

"*In the body.*" The Apostle did not forget that it might be said to all believers, " Having therefore these promises, beloved, let us cleanse ourselves from all defilement of *flesh and spirit;* perfecting holiness in the fear of the Lord " (2 Cor. vii. 1). Still he had, in accordance with a profound physiology and philosophy, strong ideas in reference to the mighty influence of the body on the spirit. In some respects the spirit nobly dominates the body; in others the body rudely thrusts itself into the foreground

of influence, and the spirit, instead of dominating, is ignobly dominated.   The 20th verse
of the 6th chapter of the 1st Epistle to the
Corinthians runs thus in our public English
version: "Ye are bought with a price : therefore glorify God *in your body, and in your spirit,
which are God's.*"   But in the more correct text,
given by the critical Editors, and accepted by
the Revisionists, the exhortation runs thus : "Ye
were bought with a price : glorify God therefore
in your body."   Far-reaching ethical results are
determined by the body.   Hence the Apostle's
entreaty in a succeeding part of the Epistle
to his fellow-Christians in Rome, "I beseech
you therefore, brethren, by the mercies of God,
to present your *bodies* a living sacrifice, holy, and
acceptable to God, your rational service" (xii. 1).
If the body be laid upon the altar of consecration,
the 'informing' spirit will not be withheld.   If
sin be not allowed to reign *in the body*, there
is but little likelihood of its iron sceptre being
reverenced *in the spirit*.

εἰς τὸ ὑπακούειν ταῖς ἐπιθυμίαις αὐτοῦ.   It is impossible to render these words literally into
English.   "There are," says Dr. Jelf, "even
in classical writers, slight beginnings of the ten-
dency which we find fully developed in the Greek
of the New Testament, to confound the notions
of the aim, the cause, the result, and the infini-

tival object of a verbal notion, on the ground of their common property of following more or less closely on the verb, and their being dependent thereon " (*Gk. Gram.*, § 803). The Apostle's idea might be represented thus :—" Let not sin reign in your mortal body, *unto this being the effect, that ye obey its lusts.*" The lusts referred to are not the lusts of sin, but the lusts of the body (αὐτοῦ). They are the inordinate desires that are experienced in consciousness, in virtue of physical peculiarities interpenetrating in their effect the region of the mind. Such desires, unfed and unfanned, are not sinful. It is not sinful for them to be. Their existence is beyond the sphere of free-will. Sin begins when they are no longer controlled, restrained, denied. When not inordinate they are easily guided and are potent for good. When inordinate, and therefore "lusts," or, as the French say, *convoitises,* rather than *simple desires,* they are the wild animal in our nature, and need the strongest reins of reason and conscience laid upon their neck. It is reversing the order of nature and of God for the man to obey the lusts; the lusts should be obedient to the man.

V. 13. " *Neither present your members to be weapons of unrighteousness to sin* " (μηδὲ παρ-

ἱστάνετε τὰ μέλη ὑμῶν ὅπλα ἀδικίας τῇ ἁμαρτίᾳ).
The Apostle's figurative representations are somewhat mixed ; but they are emphatically graphic.
He does not work out complete pictures, but
contents himself with a minglement of hints and
suggestions, not rhetorically rounded off by the
help of " the wisdom of words."

In the preceding verse he had, in an earnest
hortatory spirit, lifted up a warning voice against
the reign of sin. *Let not sin reign in your mortal
body.* In this verse he retains the conception of
sin as a regnant principle. He likewise assumes
that it is actually engaged in warlike operations.
It fights for its throne : and is intolerant of
opposition. The spirit of a tyrant is in it.
Hence it seeks military submission on the one
hand, and military subsidies on the other. But,
says the Apostle, *present not your members as
weapons of unrighteousness to sin.*

In the preceding verse the mortal body is
represented as the domain over which the reign
of sin may be extended. In this the members
of the body are regarded as weapons which
may be wielded in battle, either on the side of
righteousness against unrighteousness, or on the
side of unrighteousness against righteousness.
Put them not, says the Apostle, *at the service
of sin.*

The word *members,* so far as enumeration

is concerned, would, to the writer's mind, be somewhat indefinite. The right eye would be thought of, and the right hand; the mouth also; and the tongue, and the throat—so often an " open sepulchre "; the feet likewise, which may be swift to convey either to the right place or to the wrong. The hand may be lifted up either to smite down defiant wickedness, or to shed innocent blood. Men may with their tongues either use deceit or plead the righteous cause of the widow and the fatherless. The eye may roam in wantonness, or gaze in rapture on both heaven and earth.

Take into account all the members of the body, and every man's character may be determined by the use that he makes of his physical organism. *Use it not*, says the Apostle, *in the service of sin*. Assist not the tyrant to intensify his tyranny.

" *But present yourselves to God as alive from the dead, and your members to be weapons of righteousness to God.*" ('Αλλὰ παραστήσατε ἑαυτοὺς τῷ Θεῷ ὡς ἐκ νεκρῶν ζῶντας καὶ τὰ μέλη ὑμῶν ὅπλα δικαιοσύνης τῷ Θεῷ.)

In the preceding clause the Apostle dissuades: in this he persuades. In the sphere of the former his representation is negative; in this it is positive. The two clauses are mutually complementive.

E

Present yourselves to God. There is a peculiarity in the hortatory imperative. It is
'aoristic' in tense (παραστήσατε); whereas in
the antithetical clause the tense is 'present'
(παριστάνετε). The force of the two imperatives
might be thus represented : "Neither *be ye
presenting your members* to be weapons of unrighteousness to sin; but *present yourselves at
once to God.*" Make no delay. Let there be
no indecision. If already there has been the
least wavering, let there be not a moment longer
of hesitancy. *Put yourselves instantly at the
service of God.* Tender yourselves, enlist in
His military service, and go in bravely to take
part in the "holy war" for the overthrow and
destruction of sin.

As alive from among the dead ; that is, *as
partakers of the resurrection-life of Christ.* The
Apostle calls upon his brethren to appear before
God for service, under their true colours, and in
their true character, as they really were. They
were actually, by means of faith, united to Christ.
They had been united to Him in His death. They
were now united to Him in His subsequent life,
and are heirs with Him of all the blessings and
the glory that belong to that life. Their fellow-
men around them might not recognise the reality
of such a glorious union. But God recognised
it. To Him, as well as to themselves, it was

real. To His all-seeing eye, as well as to their own self-conscious faith, they were *alive from among the vast masses of the dead*. In their every-day experience they had earnests of the grandeur of their destiny. It well became them, therefore, to be lifted up into a lofty mood of gratitude, and thus to consecrate ungrudgingly their most devoted and loyal service to their infinite benefactor.

Instead of the expression ὡς ἐκ νεκρων ζῶντας, the important uncial manuscripts א A B C read ὡσεὶ ἐκ νεκρῶν ζῶντας, and the reading has been approved of by Lachmann, Tregelles, Tischendorf (8th ed.), Alford, Westcott-and-Hort, and introduced into their respective texts. It was the reading which Theodore of Mopsuestia had before him. If it be genuine, then the idea will be as follows : " Present yourselves to God *as if* ye were alive from among the dead." It would be suggested that they had not been literally among the " dead," and that they were not now in literal union with Christ in His " resurrection-life." They were indeed, as regards privilege and prospective glory, one with Christ. But the union was ideal. It was only *as if* they had been literally " alive from the dead."

We are not disposed to accept ὡσεί as genuine. Not only is it the case that ὡς has a great preponderance of MS. authorities on its side;

it has a still greater preponderance of patristic support. It should also be borne in mind that though ὡσεί occurs frequently in the New Testament writings, it never occurs in the Epistles of St. Paul. And then, what is of very special consideration, it is more likely that a transcriber, untrammelled by strong views of verbal inspiration, should change ὡς into ὡσεί, than that he should change the uncommon ὡσεί into ὡς. A transcriber, if not dipping deep into doctrines, might be excused if he found it easier to grasp the suggestion of a rhetorical comparison, than to interpret the assertion of an ideal reality. We believe that the Apostle said, "present yourselves to God *as being really*—in Christ—*alive from the dead.*"

The Apostle is not contented with the generic exhortation,—*Present yourselves to God as alive from the dead.* He adds specifically, *and your members to be weapons of righteousness to God.* He gives prominence once more, in the spirit of plain speaking, to the constituent organs in the organism of the body. A man's character is determined by the use that he makes of these organs or members. They are the mediums through which he can operate on the world at large, and upon his fellow-men in particular. By means of them he may do good; by means of them he may do evil. God who " worketh hither-

to " is engaged in a great work. He is engaged
in a conflict too. He is the "God of Hosts,"
"mighty in battle." Confronted as He is by
legions of defiant free-wills, it is befitting that
He muster and marshal His co-operative forces
to strike the blows that are needed to put down
sin and to establish righteousness on the earth.
Hence it is likewise befitting that all who have it
in their hearts to be on the side of God, should
make tender to Him of their militant service.
Their various outer members, actuated by their
various inner faculties, are the weapons of war-
fare that are needed. Only let heed be taken that
they be wielded in the campaigns, and according
to the behests, of the Infinite Will; for then only
are the arms of precision " weapons of righteousness."

When analytically reading the words, *and your
members to be weapons of righteousness to God*,
we are mentally to carry along with us the verb
παραστήσατε. The idea is not that the weapons
are *arms of righteousness to God*. It is that, as
such arms, they are with the soldiers who wield
them, to be put at the service of God. Thus
they are to be *tendered*, or *proffered*, or *yielded*,
or *yielded up*, or *given*, or *given up*. In these
different ways has the verb been here rendered.

V. 14.   The Apostle proceeds to enforce the
injunctions of verses 12 and 13. "*For sin shall
not have dominion over you*" (ἁμαρτία γὰρ ὑμῶν οὐ
κυριεύσει).   The idea is, *for sin shall not 'lord it'
over you.* Even your own sin, accomplished reality
though it is, shall not be able to 'lord it' over
you. In general, when sin becomes an accomplished reality, it is exceedingly lordly in its
treatment of the sinner. It does not spare the
leaded lash. Under the dominion of sin, penalty
seizes hold of the infatuated sinner; and "the
way of the transgressor is hard."   The result is
that a spirit of recklessness is apt to come over
the guilty soul, and the man plunges deeper and
yet deeper into abysses of immoral indulgence
and retributive degradation.

But, says the Apostle, facing his Christian
brethren and realising the munificence of bliss
that is available to them in Christ, "sin shall not
'lord it' over you." He does not here mean,
ye shall cease from sinning. Such words indeed
are applicable in a very real import to all true
believers in Christ. But they are not applicable
to them at this particular juncture of the Apostle's
reasoning. He does not mean, *Yield not yourselves to the militant service of sin, for ye shall
be holy.* The Apostle does not thus stand still
in thought, and then simply turn round. He
holds out to his brethren in Christ a large in-

ducement, by way of motive, to constrain them to abandon unreservedly the militant service of sin, and to enlist devotedly in the militant service of God. The inducement is the double fact of (1) a holy *immunity from the retributive consequences of their sins*, and (2) a free 'enfeoffment' in the inheritance of that everlasting bliss, which is the peculiar reward of righteousness—an immunity and an 'enfeoffment' *which are the peculiar prerogatives of believers in Christ*. "Sin *shall not lord it* over you." This prerogative when realised appeals powerfully at once to the gratitude and to the moral admiration of the soul.

The Apostle proceeds, in the remainder of the verse, to explain how it is that sin, even when an accomplished fact, is not able to 'lord it' over those who believe in Christ—"*for ye are not under law, but under grace.*"

In one obvious sense all men, inclusive of believers in Christ, are *under law* (ὑπὸ νόμον). The law has authority to say to them, without any exception or distinction, *Do this ; whosoever thou art, obey my precepts.* The law is, in this respect, the voice of duty.

In like manner it may be legitimately said that all men, inclusive of the unbelieving, *are under grace.* "The grace of God hath appeared, *bringing salvation to all men*" (Tit. ii. 11). It brings salvation within the reach of every man, though it forces it upon the acceptance of no man. It thus over-arches with a possibility of glory the whole world, full as it is of wayward free-wills.

Still there is enjoyed by believers some great peculiarity of privilege, as regards both *law* and *grace*, in which unbelievers cannot, while remaining unbelieving, be participant. Believers are *not under law* inasmuch as law does not say to them,—*Do thy duty 'and live'; do it 'or die.'* And again believers are *under grace* in this peculiar respect, that God is graciously pleased, in consideration of the atoning work of Christ, to grant them the plenary remission of the penalty of their sins, and to constitute them heirs of the glory and excellency of everlasting life.

In the presence of such grand peculiarity of prerogative and privilege, it is not to be wondered at, that sin should not be able to 'lord it' over believers in Christ Jesus. And if they realise this disablement of their great enemy, great *will be* their responsive gratitude and self-consecration. *Great 'should be' their sanctification.*

Some might suppose that the expressions *under law* and *under grace* should be interpreted as having reference to a sequence of general or world-wide dispensations, which run parallel with the ages. The *dispensation of law* would, on this hypothesis, be regarded as having its centre in

Judaism, while its circumference would stretch out indefinitely till it embraced all peoples everywhere,—all peoples who were bearing on their consciences a yoke, more or less like the ' legality ' of Judaism, and consisting largely of stringent and oppressive rites and ordinances (Gal. iv. 1–11). It would then—in harmony with the world-wide interpretation proposed—be contended that " in the fulness of the time," the ritual dispensation was, as a matter of historical fact, superseded by the sunnier dispensation under which we all now live, the *Dispensation of grace*.

This chronological view, however, of the dispensations of *law* and *grace* is not the framework in which the Apostle's representation is set, in the passage before us. He is not thinking imaginatively of a time, on the one hand, when there was *law* in our human world, and no *grace*. Nor was he thinking on the other of a different time when there is grace and no law. It is not on successive ages and their ethical specialties that he is meditating. His view is more immediately practical. He is thinking of what transpires in the experience of individuals.

To each of his readers he is in substance declaring, *Thou art the man* whom I mean. When he says " *sin shall not ' lord it ' over you*," he draws attention to a peculiar ethical deliverance,

which, if eventuating at all, must happen within
the consciousness of the individual believer. *Sin*,
says he, *shall not lord it over you Roman believers.*
But sin did 'lord it' over all Roman unbelievers.
And sin still 'lords it' over all men everywhere
who are unbelievers. In all ages sin has been
lording it over unbelievers. *In all ages sin is
unable to 'lord it' over believers.*   During the
Dispensation of Judaism, it was believers only,
whether Jews or Gentiles, who were freed from
the lordliness and tyranny of their sins.   During
this present Dispensation of grace, it is believers
only, whether Gentiles or Jews, whether Greeks
or Romans, whether bond or free, who are freed
from the lordship of the law (Rom. vii. 1 ; Gal. v.
18), and who are overarched with the grace of
actual forgiveness, and acceptance, and justification, and "eternal life."   You, says the Apostle
to his Romans, are emancipated from the lordship
and lordliness of sin, because you are, since your
faith in Christ, no longer under law but under
grace.

The law exacts ; it does not give. Grace does
not exact ; it gives. The law, pure and simple,
demands the uttermost farthing of obedience and
the sum total of all possible righteousness.   It
demands, and threatens if its demands be not
complied with ; but it gives not, even to the
minutest fraction, relaxation of obligation or re-

mission of penalty. The law is not gracious, for
it is not grace. Grace is gracious. It is liberal
and generous in all its spheres. It has given
Christ " unto all," to be available to all, that He
may be available as " all their salvation." Such
is its liberality in its vastest, its all-comprehen-
sive, sphere. And, in the narrower sphere of
that community who accept the unspeakable gift,
this same Divine grace gives all the blessed elements that blend into actual salvation. Thus,
if there be any might of moral motive at all, there
is no wonder that sanctification should be the
result of the deliverance on the one hand from
the malison of the broken law, and of the acceptance on the other of the benison of "grace upon
grace."

V. 15. "*What then?*" (τί οὖν;) The Apostle has
plunged into his subject, and in the fulness of
might and mastery, is victoriously cleaving and
clearing his way now on the right hand and now
on the left. He asks *What then?* that is, *What
then should we do? What should we believers do?
What, since we are not under the dominion of law,
but under the dominion of grace?*

"*Shall we sin?*" or rather, *Should we sin?* (No
doubt we should read ἀμαρτήσωμεν with ℵ A B C D
E K L P, not ἀμαρτήσομεν, *shall we sin?* with the

Received or Elzevir Text). *Should we go on sinning? Should we go on recklessly multiplying our sins, and thus increasing our sinning?* Is that the way we should act, because, in virtue of the link of faith that unites us to Christ, " we are not under law but under grace." Notice the preposition *under*. They who are united to Christ by faith are, like others, *under authority*, but, unlike others, they are not *under the reign of law, but under the reign of grace.* Such is their new relation to the law, their Christian relation. It is peculiar; so peculiar that the law cannot now condemn them. It cannot pass sentence of condemnation against them because of their short-comings. Believers in Christ are outside the sphere of the dominion of the law, so far as the determination of their everlasting destiny is concerned. The law has no authority to say to them in reference to its precepts, *Do them or die.* Believers are within the circuit of the realm and reign of grace, so that the good things, which God, in the fulness of His grace delights to give freely, are theirs. Forgiveness is theirs. Acceptance at the bar that is before the great white throne is theirs. Eternal life is theirs. Glory, honour, and immortality are theirs. All desirable things are theirs. "All things" that can be turned into heritage are theirs, so that they can triumphantly exclaim, "All things are ours, for we are Christ's." These blessings are all theirs, because they are no longer in the sphere and under the sway of the law, but in the sphere and under the merciful and jubilant sway of grace. Should we then, in consequence of our possession of all these blessings, go on sinning? Should our immunity from the malediction of sin be seized by us as a high tower of security into which we may run, and within which we may spend our energies in the indulgence of unrestricted revel and riot?

"*God forbid*" (μὴ γένοιτο). *Far away from us be such wickedness and folly!* The Apostle abhors the idea.

V. 16. But not content with the expression of the moral nausea which was stirred within him, the Apostle proceeds to reason against the idea.

"*Know ye not,* he says, that is, surely ye do know—*that to whomsoever ye present yourselves as servants unto obedience, i.e.* with a view to obedience—*his servants ye are whom ye obey, whether of sin unto death*—sin with the result of death—*or of obedience unto righteousness*—obedience with the result of righteousness."

"There may appear," says Dr. Chalmers, "a sort of unmeaning and uncalled-for tautology in this verse, a something not very close or conse-

quential, and which it is difficult to seize upon "
(*Lectures on Romans*, in loco). There is certainly no refined " wisdom of words," nothing
of the nature of rhetorical artifice in the nice
adjustment of clause to clause. But there is a
great grappling with great ideas, and an earnest
application of them to the conscience.

" Know ye not " ? says he. He addresses his
readers as if they were his hearers, ignoring the
intervenience of pen and ink. And his address is
not so much in the spirit of a philosophic theo-
logian, as in the mood and manner of a practical
moralist. He *deals* with them, and speaks very
much as he would address and exhort, around the
hearth of some home, a company of Christian
friends. When he says, " Know ye not," he
assumes that the idea, which he is about to em-
phasise, is really unchallengeable ; and yet, as he
correctly judges, it may be profitably considered,
and considered iteratingly and re-iteratingly.

The drift of what he emphasises is this,—
*When any ethical course of conduct is deliberately
chosen and pursued, then the naturally retributive
consequences necessarily stereotype themselves in
the experience of the individual.* If the course
chosen be righteous, then the consequences within
the sphere of consciousness are pleasant and
tend to bliss. Whereas if the course of procedure
be at variance with the absolutely perfect stan-

dard of righteousness, the absolutely perfect will, then the consequences in consciousness rasp sooner or later on the most sensitive elements in the heart of the being, and tend to terminate in penal disharmony and unspeakable distress.

The Apostle, however, brings out his idea in figurative form, and, when thus brought out, he handles it, not in the way of abstract proposi- tions, but concretely in the way of thrusting the consideration of it home to the business and bosom of every one of his readers.

" *To whomsoever ye present yourselves to be ser- vants.*" It is assumed that all men are servants and must be servants. They are under authority, whether they recognise the fact or not. No man is supreme in relation to himself. Every man has a master. While every man can choose, his elective range is strictly within limits ; and ac- cording as he chooses, some Power or other beyond himself controls the effect of his choice. In choosing he may elect to be under the control of the one or the other of two opposing ethical principles. But between the two he must make choice. Both are master-principles so far as the ethical regulation of life is concerned. But they are moral contraries. The Apostle figura- tively represents them as Lords or Masters. They rule the life so far as retribution is con- cerned.

Well, "to whomsoever ye present yourselves
to be servants,"—*i.e.* to whichsoever of the two
Masters ye consecrate the service of yourselves,
" with a view to obedience," *i.e.* under the free
determination to do what is in harmony with
the regulative principle that has been chosen.
The Apostle puts it figuratively and concretely
thus,—" to whichsoever Master ye freely present
yourselves to be servants with a view to habitual
obedience." Then he proceeds to aver that "his
servants ye are whom ye obey." There is only
the appearance of tautology, for while it is one
thing to offer or present oneself to be an obedient
servant, it is another thing altogether, though
intimately related, to be accepted as a servant
for obedience and treated accordingly. It is one
thing to choose your regulative principle, and
another thing altogether to be retributively regulated by it when once it is chosen. Choice, and
the retributive consequences of choice, are not
to be confounded. Whatever the latter are, they
are not human choices. " His servants ye are
whom ye obey." The master controls the life.
And consequently whatever the character of the
master, thus will the servants be treated. If the
master be good, the treatment of the servants
will be fair and benign. If the master be tyrannous and selfish and evil, his treatment of the
servants will be tyrannical and oppressive.

Hence the Apostle adds, distinguishing the two opposing master-principles, " whether of sin unto death, or of obedience unto righteousness." Such is the great ethical alternative ; and it is final. Men must be servants either of *sin* or of *obedience*. In these ethical fundamentals there is no middle ground of neutrality. By *obedience*, which is in itself a neutral term applicable alike to the servants of sin and the servants of holiness, the Apostle here means *obedience proper* on the part of men, that is, obedience to goodness, and to the preceptive will of God. All other obedience, so called, obedience to that which is opposed to the will of God, is *disobedience proper*.

Men then are servants either of sin or of obedience. If of sin, the consequence is that they are dealt with according to the nature of the master. He gives his servants "wages" for their maintenance; but the wages are "death" (ver. 23). They are the destruction of the weal, peace, and bliss of the soul. If, on the other hand, men are the servants of obedience, and are thus controlled by the spirit of obedience, then they are treated according to the essential nature of obedience and righteousness, and thus of the righteous God, the holy, just, and good.

The Apostle's use of the word "obedience" is somewhat peculiar. We naturally look upon "obedience" as being the characteristic of a

F

servant rather than of a master. But here *it is* itself the Master who is to be obeyed. There is perfect logical propriety in the representation. *Obedience is the true antithesis of Sin, for sin is disobedience.* Since sin, then, is one of the dominating principles, it is fitting that obedience should be the other. Men must either be obedient or sin. If they be voluntarily and deliberately characterised by "obedience," they will be treated according to the nature of that great and good regulative principle. They shall have a reward of bliss. But if they voluntarily and deliberately yield themselves to the service of disobedience, or sin, then they must submit to be dealt with according to the nature of the master to whom they have presented the service of their members.

There is not a direct antithesis between the expressions "sin unto death" and "obedience unto righteousness." A direct antithesis would be secured if we were to balance the clauses thus, "sin unto death" and "obedience unto life everlasting." But the Apostle is satisfied with the indirect mode of antithesis; and it affords him the opportunity of emphasising the idea of sanctification. Ethical obedience, when voluntarily and deliberately yielded to God, results in "righteousness." It is, says the Apostle, "unto righteousness."

V. 17. "*But thanks be to God that ye were servants of sin.*" It is a peculiar expression, redolent of literary felicity. The Roman brethren *had been* servants of sin. But this unhappy servitude was now a thing of the past. " Troja fuit." It is as if the Apostle had said, " Ye *were*, but are not now, *servants of sin.*" They had addicted themselves to the unholy service; and as a fitting penal consequence sin had dealt with them according to its immutably evil nature. It handled them roughly; and, domineering over them, caused them to suffer *in* their service, and caused them to suffer *for* their service. There is, whether men recognise it or not, something of ineradicable unrest, uneasiness, and sorrowfulness in sin. All wickedness has woe in its heart.

"God be thanked," says the Apostle, that your service to sin is past. He sees the hand of God in their emancipation. It did not work necessitatingly indeed, or violently or capriciously; yet it actually worked; graciously and compassionatingly and effectually. The Apostle was as thankful as if the whole blessing had been emptied into his own lap, and had been for his own special enjoyment and indeed for himself alone. *God be thanked, i.e.* let God be thanked; by you, my Roman brethren, and by me. It is my desire that thus God should be thanked.

It is meet that His working should be apprehended and appreciated.

" *Ye obeyed from the heart the form of teaching
into which ye were delivered.*" Here is the true
reason for the thankfulness of the Apostle ; and
the reason why the Romans themselves should
be actuated by intensity of gratitude, A revo-
lution had taken place in their mode of life and
in the ethical aims by which they were actuated.
They had become, in their character, converted
persons, and their conversion had been effected
through the instrumentality of some peculiar
kind of Divine evangelical " teaching."

The evangelical teaching referred to was of
a certain " type." That is the word which is
employed by the Apostle (τύπος). There was in
the reality represented by the word a certain
distinct *impress*, which *stamped* its similitude
upon the recipient mind, and thus presented such
bold outlines of evangelical idea as sufficed for
the ethical transformation and transfiguration of
the life. The *impress*, so far forth as incomplete reality would permit, *expressed* the essence
of the gospel in its grand ethical potency. The
Apostle signalises the result. *The Roman brethren
obeyed the type of teaching into whose educative
influence they had been handed over.* Hence
their conversion ; their holiness. It was a
monument to the power of Divine instruction,

even when that instruction was only partially developed.

It should not be assumed that in the expression *the type of doctrine into which ye were delivered* there is a reference to full-orbed evangelical truth, or to the gospel in its maturity. The Roman brethren in general had not enjoyed the privilege of detailed apostolic teaching. No apostle had ever visited them. But they had been taught the first great principles of Christianity; and they had turned to good account such incomplete teaching as they had enjoyed. Their type of teaching had been to a large extent a thing at second hand, or at some still farther remove from the primal source. In many departments of thought there would probably be numerous intervening links between what they themselves had heard on the one hand, and what had been elsewhere spoken by the lips of the apostles on the other.

But yet *they had obeyed from the heart such type of doctrine as had been brought within their reach.*

The construction of the sentence is somewhat irregular. The expression τύπον διδαχῆς exhibits a case of 'grammatical attraction.' Had it not been for the perturbation consequent on this attraction we might have expected the statement to have run thus, ὑπηκούσατε δὲ ἐκ καρδίας τῷ τύπῳ τῆς διδαχῆς εἰς ὃν παρεδόθητε.

The clause " into which ye were delivered "
seemed so peculiar to our translators and Castellio
and many other expositors, that they assigned to
it an impossible construction and interpretation,
rendering it *which was delivered to you,* instead
of *into which ye were delivered.* The Apostle's
idea, however, is, that his Roman brethren had
been heartily obedient to the peculiar type of
doctrine into whose educative influence they had,
in the gracious Providence of God, been handed
over. The result had been most satisfactory.
By yielding themselves heartily to such teaching
of the gospel as was within their reach, they
remained no longer in the service of sin. The
life they were now living in the flesh, in hope
of the glory of God, was a new and holy life of
determined antagonism to unrighteousness, and
of devoted consecration to righteousness and to
God.

Some critics, inclusive of Beza, Tholuck, Bishop
Wordsworth, and Dr. Chalmers have supposed
that, when the Apostle speaks of *a type of teaching into which believers are delivered,* he draws
his figurative representation from metallurgy, and
particularly from the casting or moulding of
metals. Bishop Wordsworth gives the import
of the passage thus : " You readily obeyed the
mould of Christian faith and practice, into which
at your baptism you were poured as it were,

like soft, ductile, and fluent metal, in order to
be cast and take its form. You obeyed the
mould; you were not rigid and obstinate, but
were plastic and pliant and assumed it readily."
" The metaphor," he continues, " suggested itself
to the Apostle in the city where he was writing
this Epistle, Corinth, famous for casting statues,
etc., in bronze." This interpretation evokes so
vivid a representation of imagery that there is
no wonder that it should have thrown a spell
of fascination over numerous minds. But it is
nevertheless an improbable exegesis. It is somewhat violent to represent believers as *obeying*,
and *obeying from the heart, a mould of teaching
into which they were run.* The idea of freedom
is prominently involved in the conception of
ethical *obedience;* but it is lost in the conception
of a metallurgical *casting into a mould.* The
Apostle thanks God that his Romans had *obeyed.*
It would by no means have been an unparalleled
case had they disobeyed. But the idea of such
possible disobedience is obliterated the moment
that we think of them as cast into a metallurgic
mould.

V. 18. "*And, being emancipated from sin,
ye became devoted to the service of righteousness.*" (ἐλευθερ*ν*θέντες δὲ ἀπὸ τῆς ἁμαρτίας ἐδουλώθητε

τῇ δικαιοσύνῃ.) Such was the happy result of obeying the type of evangelical teaching into which they had been initiated. The fetters which sin had laid upon them were snapped, and they themselves, animated by the mightily constraining sympathy and love of the Redeemer, had "struck the blow." They ceased to work for sin. "Cease to do evil,—learn to do well," said God by the mouth of Isaiah the prophet. The Apostle's Romans followed out the Divine instruction. There is not any explicit reference to Divine redemption, or to a ransom, or to propitiation. These belong to different cartoons of representation, invaluable "for instruction" in their own places, but not requiring to be monopolisingly obtruded into every place. The peculiar experiences of the Apostle's Romans are here, so far as details are concerned, hidden behind the one great fact of their emancipation or freedom. They were free, and they knew it. They had been sin's servants; and as sin is a tyrant, they had been its slaves. In working for their cruel taskmaster they had been constrained to work in fetters, and under the uplifted rod of the oppressor. It was severely irksome work, as well as ignominious service. Figure apart, they had found in their conscious experience that sinning, even in its most defiant moods and revels, is wearisome work, unsatisfying, un-

comfortable, full of heart-aches and of a sense
of shame. "At last it is sure to bite like a
serpent and to sting like an adder." Such had
been the experience of the Roman believers in
the days of their darkness and unbelief. But
they came under the influence of "the truth
that makes free," and, "being freed from the
slavery of sin, they devoted themselves to the
service of righteousness." Service of one kind
or another was with them, as it is with all men,
an ethical necessity. Man must serve, as we
have again and again seen; but it is man's prerogative to choose his Master. The emancipated
Romans freely gave themselves up to the service
of "Righteousness."

The Apostle might have varied his pictorial
representation. He might have represented the
Master as Holiness, or as Obedience, or as Love,
or as Goodness, or as God. The supreme Master
is certainly God. But if the attention be with-
drawn from the Infinite Personality, and turned
instead to the consideration of the Master-
principle in things ethical, then there may be the
choice of any one of the other representations.
The Apostle chooses *Righteousness*, a perfect im-
personation of the Supreme Imperative within
the conscience. They only are ethically "right,"
whose inner and outer demeanour is regulated
by the dictates of "Righteousness." The entire

career of our Saviour, who left us a spotless example, was a service of Righteousness.

V. 19. "*I speak after the manner of men be-cause of the infirmity of your flesh.*" (Ἀνθρώπινον λέγω διὰ τὴν ἀσθένειαν τῆς σαρκὸς ὑμῶν.) The Apostle, in view of what he had just been saying in the preceding verse, and of what he was about to add in the clauses that immediately follow, seems to have felt that his representations were far from being of the highest possible order of thought. They were not conceived and wrought out on the loftiest possible plane of pictorial embodiment. Hence he, as it were, apologises for them, and says, *I speak what is human, I speak humanly* (the expression is an instance of the adverbial accusative). It is assumed that there is a diviner style of thinking and speaking on such subjects. Man indeed, cannot, in his standpoints of thought, transcend his own atmosphere. His thoughts, subjectively considered, *must be "human."* But objectively contemplated, they may be flashes from above. God is a Revealer, and is con-stantly revealing to the percipient and recipient spirit. The more willing and docile the spirit may be, the more, and still the more will be the compass of the receptivity. The Apostle's recep-tivity was pre-eminently large. And to him "God

made revelation through the Spirit" (1 Cor. ii.
10). "He had received," he tells us, "not the
spirit of the world, but the spirit which is of
God; that he might know the things that are
freely given to us by God" (1 Cor. ii. 12).
When it was fitting, he could "speak wisdom
among the perfect" (2 Cor. ii. 6). But many of
his brethren were "babes in Christ," to whom
"he could not speak as unto spiritual, but as
unto carnal" (1 Cor. iii. 1). He had "to feed
them with milk, not with meat" (1 Cor. iii. 2).
Their intelligence was comparatively undevel-
oped on the ethical side of their understanding.
Hence those rather homely and inæsthetic Pre-
sentations or Impersonations of *service yielded
to sin*, to *impurity*, to *lawlessness*, on the one
hand, and to *righteousness*, *holiness*, and *obedience*, on the other. Strictly speaking, there are
no such masters. Strictly speaking, sin is not
a tyrant, nor is a sinner the tyrant's slave.
The true nature of sin cannot be understood
unless in the light of volition and choice and
freedom and responsibility. But such is the
milk which the Apostle gave to his Roman
brethren. M. le Cene seized the spirit, though
he left the exact lines, of the Apostle's apolo-
getic expression, when he rendered the parenthesis thus :—*I speak 'popularly' because of the
infirmity of your body.*

The word *body* is not quite a happy substitute for the word *flesh*. The one did not entirely replace the other. And the Apostle having both the words before him (verse 6), chose *flesh*, for this reason among others—that more than *body*, it had got idiomatic attachments of ethical significance. The fundamental import, however, of both the terms is essentially identical. Men, in their higher relations, are apt to be repressed and oppressed, and kept from soaring aloft, by reason of the imperious earthward appetences of the incarnated condition. There is apt to be more of the animal than of the angel in human self-consciousness.

The phrase, *infirmity of the flesh*, means, not the infirmity *attaching to*, but the infirmity *proceeding from*, the incarnated condition. Webster says : " The genitive in its primary meaning appears to denote an object *from which something proceeds* " (*N. Test. Syntax*, p. 63).

The Apostle, it will be noted, does not say *because of the infirmity of 'my' flesh*, or even *because of the infirmity of 'our' flesh*. He could, no doubt, in other circumstances, have readily stooped to make such an abasement of himself. But at present he was strong in the consciousness of Divine illumination. He knew that he was taught by God. And he knew moreover that, as a matter of fact, he had been seeking

out such representations as would be most easily
apprehended, and most readily turned to practical account, by his brethren in Rome.

He proceeds to inculcate that species of service
that is right and pure and noble; and he lays
down for guidance the minimum measure of
devotedness. He says, " for as ye presented your
members servants to impurity and iniquity unto
iniquity, so now present your members servants
to righteousness unto holiness." (ὥσπερ γὰρ
παρεστήσατε τὰ μέλη ὑμῶν δοῦλα τῇ ἀκαθαρσίᾳ καὶ
τῇ ἀνομίᾳ εἰς τὴν ἀνομίαν, οὕτως νῦν παραστήσατε τὰ
μέλη ὑμῶν δοῦλα τῇ δικαιοσύνῃ εἰς ἁγιασμόν.)

The Apostle, vaulting over the parenthesis
which he had interposed at the commencement
of the verse, betakes himself retrospectively to
the statement made in verse 18, and consequently to that period of his brethren's experience in the time past of their lives, when they
followed their own devices, and gave a preference
to unrighteousness over righteousness. At that
period they " presented their members servants
to impurity, and to iniquity *unto iniquity*." The
members of their body, in their *tout ensemble*,
were abused by being devoted to the practice
of moral evil. But there would be variety of
degrees both in the quality and in the quantity
of the evil. All moral evil is impurity. And
all moral impurity is iniquity. It is lawlessness

(ἀνομία) in relation to the moral empire of God. There is such an ethical phenomenon as intensified and double-dyed iniquity; intensified and double-dyed impurity. There are degrees in impure thoughts, impure desires, impure intentions, impure words and works. All such impurities are in their entirety "impurity." And all moral impurity is factiousness, lawlessness, and rebellion in relation to God.

In times past the Apostle's Romans had unblushingly yielded up voluntarily the various members of their bodies as servants to sin. They knew that they had. The Apostle knew that they knew. And both he and they knew what had been the result of such bad and base devotement of themselves. It was certainly no very great enjoyment and "gaiety." It was simply "iniquity." They "yielded up their members to uncleanness, and *to iniquity unto iniquity*." That was the honest result. Almost all that was really pleasant in the "pleasures of sin" might have been enjoyed apart from sin's uncleanness and iniquity. Pleasure is one thing, sin itself is a totally different thing. It is not needful that they be commingled in order that the pleasure may be enjoyed. The pleasure may be had "neat." The happiness that is in riot and revelry might almost always be obtained without the riot and the revelry, without being asso-

ciated with and contaminated by the presence
of uncleanness. " Stolen waters are sometimes
sweet; " but waters got without theft are
sweeter still. The sweetness in the poisoned
cup would be none the less, but all the more, if
the poison were left out. The romp would be all
the more delightful if the revel were eliminated.
It was well, therefore, that the Apostle did not
say, " Ye presented your members servants to
impurity and iniquity *resulting in a life of gaiety
and pleasure.*" It is well that he said, " Ye
presented your members servants to impurity
and iniquity, *resulting in iniquity.*" That, that,
when the robe of illusion is stripped off, is the
naked result. When impurity was chosen, sweet
enjoyment was anticipated. But no. The vati-
cination of the fond heart was a false prophecy.
The only result was iniquity. The sinner was
left alone with his sin.

But the Apostle is referring to past impurity
and iniquity unto iniquity, in order to set over
against so dark a picture the brightness of the
holy kind of life which he desired for his brethren
in Rome and throughout the world. " *So present
your members to the service of righteousness unto
holiness.*" We might have expected that he
would have formulated the antithesis thus—
" For *as ye formerly presented* your members to
the service of impurity unto iniquity, *so have ye*

now presented your members to the service of righteousness unto holiness." This affirmation of an actual historical fact is the kind of statement that we should have expected in confirmation of the assertion embodied in the 18th verse : " Being freed from sin, *ye became* servants of righteousness."

But the Apostle, in the second clause of the statement, which is his ' burden ' in this 19th verse, lets stand aside all mere confirmatory affirmation, and strides forward in the spirit and mood of one who is the bearer of a grand ethical imperative ($\pi a \rho a \sigma \tau \dot{\eta} \sigma a \tau \epsilon$) ; he strides forward till he stands face to face with his Romans, and unburdens his spirit in an emphatic injunction of sanctification. " *Present now your members to the service of righteousness unto holiness.*" The desire of the Apostle's heart glowed into a whiteheat of intensity to the effect that his fellowbelievers should be walking, though at an unmeasured distance behind, in the footsteps of Him who was "holy, harmless, undefiled, and separate from sinners "—sinners in the emphatic signification of the term.

V. 20.   " *For when ye were servants of sin ye were free in relation to righteousness.*" ($\ddot{o} \tau \epsilon \ \gamma \grave{a} \rho$ $\delta o \hat{\nu} \lambda o \iota \ \ddot{\eta} \tau \epsilon \ \tau \hat{\eta} s \ \dot{a} \mu a \rho \tau \acute{\iota} a s, \ \dot{\epsilon} \lambda \epsilon \acute{\upsilon} \theta \epsilon \rho o \iota \ \ddot{\eta} \tau \epsilon \ \tau \hat{\eta} \ \delta \iota \kappa a \iota o \sigma \acute{\upsilon} \nu \eta.$)

Let the conjunctive *for* at the commencement of the statement be noted. It is the link that connects the contents of the verse with the contents of the second part of the preceding verse. The Apostle had just inculcated on his Romans the duty of presenting their members as " servants to righteousness unto holiness." And now, he adds, as confirmatory of his injunction, "*for* when ye were in the service of sin, ye were free in relation to righteousness." It is as if he had said, "*I do well to urge upon you the service of righteousness unto holiness, for assuredly the very fact that formerly ye did nothing of the kind is a reason why you should improve your present opportunity.*"

The expression *free in relation to righteousness* is somewhat peculiar as meaning something evil, and consequently something that should not be. But we may learn from it, that it is not all freedom that is good. Freedom is a charming word. There is a sort of magic and bewitching glamour in it. The whole world loves it, and pants after the great reality of which it is the symbol. Nevertheless it is not all freedom that is good. In the expression " free in relation to righteousness," there is reference made to an evil freedom. When the Apostle's Romans were the servants of sin, they were " free from righteousness." They then possessed a rude, and

G

wretched, and most undesirable freedom. Indeed, unlimited or absolute freedom is an impossibility to creatures; and to desire it is to desire the annihilation of a creature's condition. When, moreover, men enter into society, they are obliged, from the very essential nature of society, to part with portions of their freedom. In society every man is put, to a greater or less degree, under check by every other man, *i.e.* his freedom is curtailed. Now the freedom that could be enjoyed only at the expense of the blessings of society would be, not a blessed freedom, but undesirable and evil. The principle that is exemplified in society in general, is verified in all the minor societies that are included in general society. No man can enter any association whatsoever, political, ecclesiastical, economical, or literary, without paying away a part of his freedom, as the price of the benefits which the association has to offer. His connection with the association puts him more than he was before under check—it limits his freedom.

It is good for man to be thus put within limits as to freedom. Whether indeed it were good or not, it is indispensable; it is necessary. But nothing is necessary and indispensable to us that is not, all things considered, good. Man would be a creature absolutely wild, unsociable, reckless, dangerous, and, in one word, a pestilence and a nuisance, were he not to part with much of his freedom.

It is not all freedom, then, that is good. It is only such freedom as is consistent with our highest social, moral, and spiritual weal. Even the freedom wherewith Christ makes His people free is not unlimited in things spiritual and ecclesiastical. It is chiefly freedom from the penalty, freedom from the condemnation, and freedom from the defilement of sin. It is freedom the reverse of that license which unbelieving men cherish and assert, and which is signalised by the Apostle, when he says, in the words before us, "when ye were the servants of sin, ye were free from righteousness," *i.e.* ye were free in relation to righteousness, ye kept yourselves unengaged in reference to righteousness,—ye did not use your members in subordination to the behests of the master-principle of Righteousness. It is likewise worthy of being noticed, that as unbelievers experience freedom from righteousness only when they lay down their freedom in relation to sin, and yield themselves servants to sin; so whensoever *any* undesirable and evil freedom is experienced, it is invariably realised at the expense of freedom that is desirable and good. They who are free from righteousness are not free from sin. It is because they renounce their freedom in reference to sin, and yield themselves servants in reference to sin, that they are "free from righteousness." They again, who are "servants to righteousness," are free from sin. They have a blessed freedom. Human nature is so constructed that if a man will sacrifice some of the highest blessings of which he is susceptible, in order that he may not part with his freedom, he will, in the very sacrifice that he makes, bring himself under bondage to evils, and thus rob himself of a far nobler freedom than he retains. In our Public version—King James's—the phrase is rendered *free from righteousness.* Not quite felicitously, inasmuch as such a translation seems to suggest that righteousness has claims from which a man may be free. There is no such freedom.

The word *free* when employed in reference to servants and service, naturally enough denotes *disengagement.* While the Apostle's Romans were servants of sin, they were *not engaged to righteousness.* They were unengaged in relation to righteousness. They could not at the same time be servants both to Righteousness and to Unrighteousness. It is one of the old, old stories. "No man can serve two masters," when these masters are mutually antagonistic. The Apostle's Romans came under the sweep of the great Teacher's apophthegm, and so, at the bypast time referred to, they criminally held back their hand

and their heart from engaging in the service of righteousness. The freedom they used was freedom abused.

V. 21. " *What fruit then had ye at that time ?* " (τίνα οὖν καρπὸν εἴχετε τότε;) Note the connecting *then*. It intimates that the Apostle puts his query in view of the statement that goes immediately before, viz. that his Romans, in their former and unconverted state, had rendered no service of consecration to Righteousness. " What fruit then had ye at that time ?" Note the word *fruit*. Its normal meaning is *natural vegetable product*. It is, of course, primarily a botanical term, and may, when peculiarly qualified, denote products that are deleterious, as well as products that are wholesome. Such outgrowths, however, are exceptional. The immense preponderance of fruits is good and salubrious, so that the word *fruit*, unless otherwise defined, limited, or qualified, naturally denotes that which is good and desirable for eating, or, it may be, what is positively delicious. " *Unfruitful* works of darkness" (Eph. v. 11), are not works utterly destitute of results, but works that are barren of beneficent or beneficial results. And in the case before us, the Apostle, in his survey, finds no outcome that is good. Hence his query

"What fruit had ye at that time?" Some
critics conceive that the query is complete as it
thus stands. What immediately follows (ἐφ' οἷς
νῦν ἐπαισχύνεσθε) they regard as the answer to the
query, "What fruitage then had ye? [*Things*]
of which ye are now ashamed." This, as is
evidenced by the punctuation of their texts, is
the view taken by both Lachmann and Tischendorf. But it is more natural to postpone the
interrogation point, so that the two clauses combined may form a single query, as in our public
English Version and the Revision ;—"What fruit
then had you at that time [from those things]
of which you are now ashamed?" Had you,
in any of them, a single drop of pure enjoyment? Was the conscience ever satisfied? Was
the heart? Such questions are pertinent. It is
as if the Apostle had said, *You never had any
sweet fruit of happiness at all.* How could you,
when the blight of God's anathema was blowing
into hurricane upon your vices? "For," says
the Apostle, "the end of those things is death."
(τὸ γὰρ τέλος ἐκείνων, θάνατος). By the word *death*
he means something altogether different from, or
at all events, something far more generic than
natural decease, or the mere termination of
terrestrial existence. There is ultimately indeed
that termination in the case of all, whether good
or evil, whether obedient or disobedient. But the

existence, whithersoever transferred, and wheresoever spent, is ever more than mere existence.
It is existence in the midst of peculiar environ-
ment; existence with all the flowers of happiness
culled out, or crushed down. It is existence
over-run with unwholesomeness and weeds, or
thick-strewn with thorns and thistles and other
abominations. The death referred to is *the penal
destruction of well-being.* That destruction is the
natural termination and end of all shameful, and
in particular of all shameless doings.

V. 22. "*But now being emancipated from sin,
and devoted to the service of God, ye have your
fruit unto holiness, and the end everlasting life.*"
(νυνὶ δὲ, ἐλευθερωθέντες ἀπὸ τῆς ἁμαρτίας, δουλωθέντες
δὲ τῷ Θεῷ, ἔχετε τὸν καρπὸν ὑμῶν εἰς ἁγιασμόν, τὸ δὲ
τέλος ζωὴν αἰώνιον.) The great change, ever since
you believed in the Lord Jesus, has established
itself in your experience. "You are new creatures." "Old things have passed away; behold
all things have become new." You are no longer
the willing slaves of sin. You have become the
willing servants of God, without a single in-
gredient either of slavery or reluctance in your
service. In His service you enjoy your highest
freedom, for the service of God has in it no
element of constraint or compulsion, over-riding

the willinghood of the soul. As the result of
such service, *you have an outcome of fruit;* you
have *your fruit,* your fitting and normal fruit,
ripening into richest result. It is fruit issuing
in holiness. That is the ripest and richest result;
and then the end of the whole life of probation
and discipline on earth, is eternal life in glory,
the endless life of bliss, that life which is at
present " hid with Christ in God."

V. 23. "*For the wages of sin is death; but the
gift of God is life eternal in Jesus Christ our Lord.*"
(τὰ γὰρ ὀψώνια τῆς ἁμαρτίας θάνατος, τὸ δὲ χάρισμα
τοῦ Θεοῦ ζωὴ αἰώνιος ἐν Χριστῷ Ἰησοῦ τῷ Κυρίῳ ἡμῶν.)

The Apostle confirms the affirmation which
he made in the preceding verse. Hence the
reason-rendering " for." Man's future is retributive. It will be what it will be, in virtue of the
man's peculiarity *in things present.* The future
is begotten by the present.

The Apostle carries out his favourite imperson-
ation. He paints into a picture his vivid ideas.
Sin once more stands out objectively on his
canvas as an evil master, a domineering lord, an
absolute tyrant. The picture is an appropriate
hieroglyph. There is something ineradicably
savage in sin. Were it alive and self-conscious,
it would feel itself taking pleasure in torturing

and tormenting. Its ways are the blood-stained paths of relentless exaction and oppression. Wheresoever service is rendered, there will retribution be meted out according to the essential nature of the master who is served. The retribution earned by persisted-in sin, is the wages which the tyrant gives to his serfs. The Apostle has carried his pictorial idea as far as his pictorial imagery will stretch. Other masters give "wages" for the maintenance of their servants. Even the utterly selfish and unfeeling, who wield a mercilessly leaded lash, and who grudge the very rags that can be hung in tatters on the persons of their slaves; even these give *supplies* (ὀψώνια) to prolong the term of life, and thus the term of servitude. But sin has the bad pre-eminence of paying its serfs by punishing them. Its ὀψώνια— its wages—are death, and the death for which its counters are available, is the destruction of the weal of the soul.

Such is the retribution of those who persist in sinning. Such is the lurid gloom of the picture which is held up for inspection and reprobation. A voice says *"look on this side and on that."* But contrariwise when we turn, and look, not on *that*, but on *this*, the contrast picture, we see with a feeling of ethical elevation, and of "joy unspeakable," that the retribution of the believing, their 'award' and 'reward,' is overarched with a Divine glory. God, the Divine Master, does not give *wages* (ὀψώνια) at all; or, if He does, then His liberal *wages*, ere they pass from His full hand into the empty hands of His faithful servants, become transfigured into something better far. He gives, out of His own unpurchasable munificence, a free gift of bliss. It is "life everlasting." It is happiness perennial and eternal. It was the reward of Jesus, after He finished His work in agony and woe, and was buried, and then rose again and ascended. It is still the unexhausted and inexhaustible reward which Jesus is enjoying, and will enjoy for ever and ever. The same reward is ours, the moment that union with Christ is ours. Let any man be so closely united to Christ, that "to him to live is Christ" day after day of his probationary existence, and then there is no evil influence in all the Universe that can separate him from the love of God. "Eternal life is his in his Lord Jesus Christ."

APPENDIX.

I.

ADDITIONAL NOTES ON ROMANS VI. 14.

In Romans vi. 14, the Apostle brings to view a peculiar relationship of those who have received the gospel. He says, "*Sin shall not have dominion over you, for ye are not under Law but under Grace.*"

"Over you"—you, that is to say, who have welcomed into your hearts the gospel.

How could the Apostle so express himself, when he was prepared to say in the 1st verse of the next chapter, "Know ye not, brethren, that the law has dominion over the man as long as he lives?"

To what law does he refer?

It is well to bear in mind that in the Apostle's writings the term has a somewhat varied range of reference. It sometimes denotes *the whole of the Old Testament Revelation*. Most appropriately so, for that Revelation was really, in its sum-total, an Authoritative Revelation of the will of God.

Sometimes the word denotes that portion of the Old Testament Revelation which is comprised in *the Pentateuch*.

Sometimes the Psalms and the Prophets are added, in thought, to the Pentateuch, and then all together constitute *one complex Law*.

Sometimes there is a condensation of the reference, representing at one time the essential duty of man as man, or more expansively, at another, the duties, pre-rogatives, and privileges of Jewish men as Jews.

The Apostle, in using the term, employs it as a great and comprehensive thinker might be expected to employ it, realising the complexity involved in its unity. He hence contemplates the complex object at very various angles of vision. And, as was not unnatural, he fre-quently shifts his standpoint, moving rapidly round the object of his contemplation, and looking at it in a suc-cession of its manifold aspects. Unless we bear in mind that, in speaking of *the Law*, the Apostle was thus deal-ing with a many-sided unity, we shall be often perplexed when we try to follow in the train of his discussions.

It is demonstrable that in Romans vi. 14, and in Romans vii. 1 and 6, the Apostle refers to the Law, viewed as an Authoritative Revelation of the will of God *in reference to man, as man*. He is, in other words, referring to the Law in that one central aspect of its entirety, which is frequently, and excellently, designated *the Moral Law*. It is the Decalogue, *i.e.* the ten words or ten commandments. Or it is the duologue, *i.e.* the two words, the two commandments :—Supreme-love-to-God, and Love-to-our-neighbour-such-as-we-bear-to-our-selves.

That it is the decalogue or duologue that is referred to in the passages before us, is evidenced by Romans vii. 7—" *What shall we say then ? Is the Law sin ? Away with that thought* (Μὴ γένοιτο) *! I had not known sin but through the Law ; for I had not known coveting except the Law had said, Thou shalt not covet.*" The Apostle's quotation points to the law he had been signal-ising, and identifies it as distinctly and demonstratively as his reference in Chapter xiii. 8, 9, where he says, " Owe no man anything but to love one another; for he that loveth another hath fulfilled *the Law*." What Law ?

The Decalogue; for the Apostle goes on to say—"For this, Thou shalt not commit adultery, Thou shalt not kill, Thou shalt not steal, Thou shalt not bear false witness, Thou shalt not covet, and if there be any other commandment, it is briefly comprehended in this word, namely, Thou shalt love thy neighbour as thyself."

Assuming that the reference of the word *Law* is as indicated, what does the Apostle mean when he speaks of this *Law* as "having dominion over a man"? He means that it has *executive power to deal with* the man as he deserves. It is not the case that the Apostle looked upon the Law as utterly powerless; defunct; a dead letter; dead or dying. It has dominion. It is alive and has power. It can lord it over the man who is subject to it; and it does so lord it. So that it still has *strength*. It is the very Law that is signalised by the Apostle in 1 Corinthians xv. 56, "The sting of death is sin; and the *strength of sin is the Law*." It is the Law that gives strength to whatsoever there is in death that has a sting. Were it not for the Law, sin would be no sin; and consequently there would be no sting in death. "Sin is the transgression of the law." *The Law then still is; and has strength, and exercises it, and dominion, and lordship.*

But if this be the case, what is meant when it is said in verse 6, "But now we are delivered from the law, *that being dead wherein we were held.*" Is there not, it may be asked, a reference in this latter expression to *the Law?* And if so, is it not expressly represented as *dead?*

In our English Version, King James's, the Law does seem unfortunately to be represented as *dead*. But in the Original Greek, as is acknowledged by all enlightened critics, without exception, it is not the Law that is represented as *dead*. It is believers in Jesus. The true translation of the Apostle's expression is given in the margin of our English Bibles, " But now we are delivered from the Law, being dead to that wherein we were held," that is, *having died and being dead to the Law.*

It is believers in Jesus who have died; not the Law. And believers are " dead," not in any dreadful sense of the term. They have died in Christ, and are dead in Christ. They " have been crucified with Christ." They died with the crucified Christ. Believers occupy, with respect to sins, the same relation which Jesus Himself now occupies. He, having died under our sins, and for them, bearing their penalty and exhausting it, " dieth no more." He is now, and for ever, free, as our Substitute, from all farther claims from the dishonoured Law—He is free from all farther liability to suffer. " Christ being raised from the dead, dieth no more." *Death has no more dominion over Him.* In His resurrection-life He " liveth unto God "—He liveth in the full enjoyment of the glorious smile of the countenance of God—a countenance that, to Him, shall never more be over-shadowed or beclouded. The darkness is past for ever. The Apostle adds—"Likewise, reckon ye also yourselves to be dead indeed to sin, and alive to God." It is thus decisively evidenced that it is not the Law that is dead, but believers, who by faith enter into Christ. Becoming parts of His person, they die in His death, and live in His life.

As regards the translation that is given in King James's English Version, " that being dead wherein we were held," its history is a little romance.

The translation rests on no manuscriptural authority whatsoever.

How then did it get itself admitted into the Elzevir Greek Testament, and into our Public English Version ? By Beza's unconscious influence.

Beza misunderstood some statements of Erasmus in

reference to some statements of Chrysostom. He says, "Erasmus being witness, Chrysostom read ἀποθανόντος (Legit igitur Chrysostomus ἀποθανόντος, Erasmo teste). It was a mistake. But Beza, having the courage of his opinions, added, "I so approve of the reading that I do not hesitate to replace it in the text." So it got a place, not in his *Annotations* only, but likewise in the text, which, in all his five editions, he places at the head of the pages. Our English Mill relieved a little his literary animus by saying, "This Annotator 'dared' to put the word into the body of the Apostolic text" (*invitis nostris libris omnibus in corpus textús Apostolici referre ausus est hic Annotator*). PROLEGOMENA cxxxi. Before the Geneva critic ventured, indeed, on the final step of elevating the mere creature of his imagination into the text, he contrived to convince himself—though in utter default of evidence—that what he fancied to be Chrysostom's reading must have been the universally accepted reading of the age (*omnino apparet eam lectionem fuisse tum sine controversia receptam*). Thus he piled blunder upon blunder, and showed himself—peculiarly strong as he doubtless was—to be weak as other men.

Several editors followed in the wake of the Elzevirs, such as Courcelles, Leusden, Schöttgen, etc. They followed blindly, however, though reverentially—not dreaming that they were presenting, as a portion of the inspired text, a reading which rests on no foundation whatever but a misunderstanding of a remark of Chrysostom. Of course Mill lifted up his protest. So did Bengel. Wetstein also, although, in accordance with his plan, he allowed the false word to remain in the text. He prefixed to it his reprobating brand. Griesbach dismissed it; and so do Lachmann, Tischendorf, Tregelles, Westcott-and-Hort, not to speak of the minor editors. Muralto fancied that ἀποθανόντος was the reading of the

Vatican. But the Vatican reads ἀποθανόντες, as does the Sinaitic. And so do all the Greek Fathers, who comment on the passage, or who quote it. There is not a speck of manuscriptural authority for ἀποθανόντος. And yet so great a man as Grotius got completely be-meshed in considering the Apostle's expression. He assumed in the first place that there was manuscriptural authority for ἀποθανόντος, and, on the basis of this assumption, he asserts the existence of the authority (*alii codices habent ἀποθανόντος*). He appeals, in the second place, to Chrysostom as having had that particular read-ing before him. And, in the third place, he says that Origen too makes mention of the reading (*cujus lectionis et Origenes meminit*), whereas Origen does nothing of the kind. So far as his mind can be gathered from Rufinus's Version—the only existing means for ascertaining his opinion—he mentions the reading that is reproduced in the Vulgate, the Itala or Older Latin, the Latin Fathers in general, and, in particular, in the manuscripts D E F G, (*Scio et in aliis exemplaribus scriptum* a lege mortis in qua detinabimur ; *sed hoc, id est,* mortui, *et verius* est et rectius) ; but he does not make the shadow of a reference to Beza's reading. (See *Opera,* vol. iv. p. 179.)

Grotius is one of those who suppose that *the Law is dead.* " Christ," says he, " in dying slew the law of Moses." Hence he construes the last clause of the 1st verse thus: " The law has dominion over a man as long as *it* lives." Wycliffe was of the same opinion. So too Eras-mus, Tyndale, Vatable. Este too, and Bengel were of the same mind. Mace likewise, and Doddridge, Taylor of Norwich, Wakefield, Newcome, Belsham, Koppe, Flatt, etc. But the great body of expositors, including Chryso-stom, Theodoret, Theophylact, Œcumenius ; Luther too, and Melanchthon, and Calvin, as well as all the chiefs of modern exegesis, construe the passage as the authors of our Public Version have done, as well as their successors, the late Revisionists. "Dieser Ansicht," as says Rückert, "sind die neusten Ausleger sammt und sonders beigetreten."

Even Beza saw that it would be utterly at variance with the scope of the paragraph to suppose that the life of the law is referred to. And, while contending that the Apostle says in verse 6th, " *That being dead,* wherein we were held," he yet does not suppose with Doddridge, Wakefield, Belsham, etc., that the Apostle meant *the law being dead.* He supposed that the meaning is, *that thing* —sin—*being dead.* He was persuaded that Paul never could say that *the law of God is dead.* (*Atqui Paulus nunquam, opinor, dicturus fuit legem Dei mortuum.*) He was right. The death of the law is an idea altogether foreign to the theology of Paul, and to the theology of all the inspired writers.

II.

LITERATURE ON ROMANS VI.

Though there is little Literature of a special description, bearing on the elucidation of *Romans* vi, still there is 'a little.' The Chapter has had, all along, a somewhat peculiar, but yet somewhat perplexing charm for such theological scholars as combined, in prominent degree, a spirit of moral earnestness with a taste for literary culture. Hence in the age of Academic Dissertations, Exercitations, Prolusions, and 'Commentations,' not infrequently was there recourse to *Romans* vi, as affording congenial material for able or elegant, as also for able *and* elegant, monographs on groups of verses, or even on single clauses and expressions. Among these

Academic Monographs, I have met with, and possess, the following :—

Jo. Conrad Auenmüller : *Quæstio Theologica utrum Mors Christo dominata fuerit?* Occasione Rom. vi. 9. (1688).

Jo. Conrad. Bauck : Dissertatio Theologica *de Morte quæ justificat a peccato.* Rom. vi. 7. (1767). An able and exhaustive Treatise.

G. Besenbeck : *De stilo gentium doctoris Paulli ad omnium hominum captum adcommodato.* Occasione Rom. vi. 19. (1759).

G. Besenbeck : Commentatio theologica exegetica *de fervido Christianorum Deo et Justitiæ sub libertatis lege serviendi studio.* Occasione Rom. vi. 19. (1760).

Fr. Kornmann : Dissertatio exegetica *de Typo apostolicæ doctrinæ digne recepto ac porro recipiendo.* Ex epistola ad Romanos vi. 17. (1730).

And. Michaelis : *De Morte ac Vita fidelium cum Christo,* ex Rom. vi. 8. (1703).

Aug. H. Niemeyer : *Commentatio in locum Paullinum* ad Rom. vi. 1–11. (1788).

Michael C. Süsserott : Exercitatio theologica *de quotidiana Christianorum morte et resurrectione.* Ex epistola ad Romanos, vi. 4, 8, et reliq. (1711).

J. Fr. Winzer : *Explanatur locus Paulli ad Romanos epistolæ* cap. vi. 1–6. (1831). Eminently scholarly.

A special niche among the Monographs should be assigned to the first half of James Fraser's Treatise entitled *The Scripture Doctrine of Sanctification.* His explication of the sixth Chapter may, for our present purpose, be detached from that of the seventh. The exegesis, though somewhat cumbrous in style, is massive, and judicious. The devoted author, minister at Alness in Ross-shire, died in 1769. His life's lot, at the commencement of his career, was cast in troublous times.

FINIS.

Butler & Tanner, The Selwood Printing Works, Frome, and London.

www.ingramcontent.com/pod-product-compliance
Lightning Source LLC
LaVergne TN
LVHW021553080426
835510LV00019B/2493